The
After
Hours

DAVID W. PLATH

The

After

Hours

Modern Japan and

the Search for Enjoyment

UNIVERSITY OF CALIFORNIA PRESS
BERKELEY AND LOS ANGELES   1969

UNIVERSITY OF CALIFORNIA PRESS
BERKELEY AND LOS ANGELES, CALIFORNIA

CAMBRIDGE UNIVERSITY PRESS
LONDON, ENGLAND

© 1964 BY DAVID W. PLATH
SECOND PRINTING, 1969
LIBRARY OF CONGRESS CATALOG CARD NUMBER: 64-16133
DESIGNED BY JANE HART
PRINTED IN THE UNITED STATES OF AMERICA

One day we shall win back Art,

       that is to say the pleasure of life;

win back Art again to our daily labour.

WILLIAM MORRIS

Acknowledgments

A novel can be written in seclusion; an ethnography can only grow from the midst of life. I have put the words to paper; I was able to do so only through the efforts of a supporting cast as great as that for a television documentary. My debts to them are many and ramified, but the chief one is to those unheadlined backers whose behind-the-scenes support has been continuous—to Lyn, Mark, and Gail.

Dr. Akanuma Shigeyoshi took my family and me into his household in Ariake in 1959 and 1960 He protected us, directed us, cared for our health, and all the while gave us a living example of the Japanese gentleman-poet in its finest form. His wife, nurse, neighbors, and kinsmen were patient and considerate of the whims of unpredictable and inquisitive outlanders. Throughout Anchiku, people opened their doors and their hearts to us.

Professor Kōhara Yukinari of the Anthropology Section, Shinshū University, Matsumoto, was a faithful advisor and companion. He has continued to help since my departure, and it was he who persuaded Mr. Yanagisawa Takeshi to prepare the illustrations for the book. The other members of the Anthropology Section, and especially Professors Suzuki Makoto and Morimoto Iwatarō, provided introductions and aid of sometimes unusual sorts. Mochizuki Kan'ichi, a history student in Shinshū, was my aide-de-camp and chief interviewer for many months; we were joined at times by another Shinshū student, Yamamoto Katsumi.

Many friends and colleagues in Tokyo furnished those personal introductions which are essential to successful fieldwork in Japan, and through conversation and consultation they greatly broadened my understanding of things Japanese. I cannot list them all, but I cannot omit the names of Professors Gamō Masao, Hoshino Akira, Hori Ichirō, Izumi Sei'ichi, Morioka Kiyomi, Sofue Takao, Takahashi Tōichi, and Yasuda Saburō. I am also grateful to two students who helped me process my field materials and who gave me many clues as to how to make sense of them, Kawada Junzō and Noguchi Takenori.

My family and I owe special thanks to Ezra F. Vogel, his wife Susan and son David—colleagues and family companions before, during, and since our stay in Japan.

The fieldwork was made possible by a Foreign Area Training Fellowship from the Ford Foundation. The Foundation also supported me in 1961 while I wrote my dissertation ("The Strung and the Unstrung: Holidays in Japanese Life," Harvard University, 1962), from which several sections of this book derive. A grant from the Institute of International Studies, University of California, Berkeley, allowed me to begin work on the book in the after hours of the summer of 1962.

An author is rarely best fitted to judge his own precious prose. I am grateful that my colleagues Delmer Brown, Dell Hymes, and Robert Murphy were willing to take on the obligations of criticizing parts of the manuscript.

Sections of this book appeared first in different form in essays and articles. I thank the publishers for permission to include materials from the following:

Asahi Shimbun-sha, Tokyo, for "Land of the Rising Sunday," *Japan Quarterly* 7:3 (July–September, 1960).

Cross Continent Co., Ltd., Tokyo, for "Overworked Japan and the Holiday Demiurge," *Today's Japan* 5:8 (August 1960).

Institute of International Studies, University of California, Berkeley, for "Will Success Spoil the Japanese?" *Asian Survey* 1:9 (November, 1961).

Association for Asian Studies, for "The Enjoyment of Daily Living: Some Japanese Popular Views," *Journal of Asian Studies* 22:3 (May, 1963).

D.W.P.

Contents

xi

1. *Introduction and Approach*

松本駅前　健

It is hard to put into words just what is involved in the fact that the combined democratic and industrial revolutions have made both workers of us all and aristocrats of us all.　LYNN WHITE, JR.

A Cultural "Opposing Self"

The modern Japanese are not easy to capture in an image. In our mind's eye we have seen them in many figures and many masks. We have seen them as peasants and poets; we have seen them as vanquished; and sometimes we have seen them as victors. Often we have seen them as sophisticated teachers come to bring us the art and wisdom of Zen. But most of all we have seen them as precocious pupils who spelled down the rest of the non-West in the contest for modernization. Theirs has been the unique story of the native who apprenticed himself in the Western workshop and left bearing the secrets of journeyman success.

But precociousness is no pure blessing: the adept must face sooner the problems of maturity. No people in today's world is secure in its provincial heritage, and none can escape our common mandate to know ourselves as partakers of a transformed human condition. As the first modernized people outside the West—and having become so largely after the manner of the West—the Japanese feel in an especially acute way the dilemmas as well as the delights of this new world environment.

My image is of the Japanese in this guise. I look at them not as apprentices but as journeyman bearers of Western skills now obliged to redefine themselves to themselves in a transformed Eastern world. My question is not—What did the Japanese do in order to modernize? Abler hands have dealt with that already, many times over. My question is—What has modernization done to the Japanese? How has it changed their efforts to maintain a meaningful, worthwhile way of living? There is an obvious sense in which men always have sought for enjoyment, but what is happening to the

2

search for enjoyment in a Japan made over by the factory, the city, the ballot box, and the eye of television?

The issue is not, of course, unique to Japan. We recognize it as pandemic in every civilization like our own that has been reshaped by the democratic and industrial revolutions. No such civilization can any longer be neatly divided into two parts, the one of working masses fit for Marx's pity, the other of leisured classes fit for Veblen's censure. For, as industrial techniques have greatly expanded the supply of Disraeli's "two civilizers of men"— increased means and increased leisure, at the same time democratic vistas have greatly increased the demand. All of us have become, simultaneously, workers and aristocrats. Before this prospect we may stand gloomy with Marx or joyful with Whitman (I suppose most of us are ambivalent), but in any case we are not likely to deny that the condition is puzzling. And neither the ideologues nor the utopians of the past provide us with prompt solutions.

The West has been assaying this condition for more than a century. Out of this effort have come ideas and concepts that today are common coinage for intellectual exchange and sometimes even for the vernacular marketing of ideas. Alienation of labor, anomie, escape from freedom, lonely crowd, organization man—all these have the smooth surface of familiar usage. But this exchange has been taking place for the most part within the bounds of the Western tradition. The very words we adopt for articulating our insights and foresights are curbed by the limits that inhere in our Indo-European linguistic apparatus.

One way to surmount these limits is to take advantage of the comparative perspective afforded by another civilization, a sort of cultural "opposing self," to use a term

Lionel Trilling coined for another purpose. At times the opposing self has been modernized and close at hand. Engels and de Tocqueville are the type cases: Engels asking what industrialization had done to the working classes in England, de Tocqueville asking what democracy had done to that new man, the American. Here the danger is that the opposing self may be so modern and familiar as to shed little contrast. At times the opposing self has been an anthropological other, an exotic, non-literate, nonindustrial, nonpopulous people. Here the danger lies in a temptation to assume that if different cultures figuratively "choose" from the "whole arc" of human variation, then all choices are equally possible; we merely have to put our wills to it and we can become Apollonian or Dionysian. At still other times the opposing self has been even more distant and ethereal, as in the arcadias of some timeless Orient or the utopias of a placeless Erewhon. And here the danger is strongest of all that hunger for reason and harmony will blind us to the unreason and disharmony of ordinary human affairs.

Modern Japan as an opposing self does not quite fit into any of these categories. It is not so Western as de Tocqueville's America, yet so like it that "non-Western" is a useless adjective. It is much too vast, literate, and industrial to be thought primitive. And it is more real than arcadia or utopia. It is no more, but no less, than living modern mankind in a Japanese visage. This is its special virtue.

Japan so seen holds a touch of irony. This is because Japan has been one of our prized specimens of arcadia ever since Marco Polo told Europe of the fabulous riches of the isles of Zipangu. Is it an accident, for example, that Japan is the only "real" country to figure in the subheadings of *Gulliver's Travels?* (Part III: A Voyage to Laputa, Balnibarbi, Luggnagg, Glubbdubdrib, and Japan). Japanese resoluteness in rejecting the West for two and a half centuries only helped whet the vision. We still are reluctant to part with it, although the realities of contact in the modern century have brought some birth-control measures to bear upon the spawning of books on "Life in Lotus-Land." We still marry Japanese brides in fiction as well as increasingly in fact. But now the spouse is not Pierre Loti's *Madame Chrysanthème*, a submissive, sloe-eyed geisha. It is James Michener's Hana-ogi (in *Sayonara*), who portrays Western roles in a girls' opera, and with whom the course of love is anything but smooth.

I have no quarrel with those who prefer an arcadian Japan. It too is a form of reality. Possibly for some soul-thirsty Americans a garbled and fragmentary Japan of Zen and ikebana is more needful than a Japan of noisome, reeking reality. After all, our era probably knows more about the Hellenic world than did the men of the Renaissance, who were historically much closer; yet we seem to draw far less inspiration from it than they did. I only state my standpoint. I find as much enchantment in, and even more to be learned from, a Japanese opposing self seen with both eyes open.

The Search for Enjoyment

If it is difficult to say just what industry and democracy involve for the human condition, it is disastrous to try to say too much. The ethnographer sees industry and democracy as great complexes of cultural traits. Industry implies not only new techniques, it implies new ties between producer and consumer, and as well new gospels of efficiency and progress. Democracy implies not only new voting methods, it implies new ties between leader and lead, and new faith that masses can be taught to make meaningful choices. These trait complexes need not congrue with the parochial cults of industry and democracy we know in the West. Perhaps our very labels carry unconscious traces of *invidium:* that industry and democracy were first made manifest in Western dress is no guarantee that they will appear elsewhere in the same form—even to the extent they have in Japan. Yet too often this is taken for granted.

I limit myself to one aspect of these many implications. It is an aspect that draws increasing attention in our day, for it is a microcosm of the wider issue. It can readily be circumscribed, though not readily trapped in a definition. It goes by several names; but I prefer the more neutral phrase "search for enjoyment." I do this to avoid intrusive connotations. "Pursuit of happiness," for example, is a phrase of classic pedigree. But "pursuit" suggests a self-conscious idealization and an almost desperate striving after specific goals; it is too rigid for the commonplace affairs I have in mind. "Contemporary hedonism" is a term favored by Georges Friedmann and some Continental sociologists. But while I am not sure what *hédonisme* means to a Frenchman I do know that its Anglo cognate hints too strongly of what Don Marquis expresses in a rolling line as "red rum ruin revolt and rapine." "Pleasure" could almost substitute for enjoyment. I avoid the word only because it brings to mind Freud's "pleasure principle" and his annoying habit— his grandchildren are beginning to cure themselves of it —of implying that all lust is in some ultimate way organic.

American critics and observers often write of "mass leisure." This term compares favorably with Lynn White's "all workers, all aristocrats," and like it recognizes the downfall of a once useful Veblennian dichotomy. But the notion of mass leisure also is muddled by differences of interpretation. To some people the term is self-contradictory: to them leisure is capital-letter Culture, the refinement and cultivation that is possible only for the few. To others the term is bogus, since even the wealthiest nation today can put its hands into pockets of poverty among its masses. To some, mass leisure means trash, tinselization, tailfins, and genius suborned by mobocracy; to others mass leisure spells the dissipation of craftsmanship and the decay of the dignity of human labor.

It is worth adding that many Japanese who write about the issue also reject stronger-sounding terms such as *kairaku* ("pleasure," "hedonism") and follow the lead of Katō Hidetoshi in using the milder *kaiteki* ("delight," "enjoyment").

The After Hours

Leisure is used as an antonym for work, and is often equated with free time or recreation or self-cultivation. My title points in this direction, toward these "after" hours, but I want to make clear that I am not rejecting work as simple oppression and unfreedom. The familiar dichotomy of work and leisure is at best misleading and a partial truth. On the one hand, it tempts us to stand narrowly with the squares, proclaiming that work is the essential purpose of living; on the other hand, to stand narrowly with the beats, asserting that life is creative leisure or it is nothing.

Western thinking has been partial to the squares. We are obliged to justify our actions in terms of economic production. The administrator and the artist

7

alike are criticized for not handling their affairs in a tough-minded, businesslike way. The bias appears in social theory as well as in popular thinking. Economics long ago won itself Carlyle's label as the dismal science. In psychiatry that Victorian square from Vienna more or less equated reality itself with the reality of the workaday world, arguing that the man who does not work loses his sense of reality and is condemned to wallow in fantasy. Again, in most theories of social evolution, changes in the productive apparatus are assumed to have necessary priority. And even the functional analysts of social organization can be overheard suggesting that "instrumental" activities are "more" functional than others. They see recreation as a social safety valve, a necessary concession to animal weakness, but otherwise practically irrelevant. The researcher who proposes to speak seriously of enjoyment—I speak from experience—often encounters the fidgety tolerance once reserved for those who would propose to speak seriously of sex.

To be sure there has been a bohemian and humanistic resistance movement holding out against the majority. But this too has often been weakened by extreme statements that tend to reject the dilemmas of work in their entirety. Among anthropologists this stance is perhaps best seen in Edward Sapir, as he writes (in "Culture, Genuine and Spurious"): "The great cultural fallacy of industrialism, as developed up to the present time, is that in harnessing machines to our uses it has not known how to avoid the harnessing of the majority of mankind to its machines," so that our daily work has become "a desert patch of merely economic effort in the whole of life."

Another difficulty with the work-leisure dichotomy is

that it applies directly to only a fraction of the population. In looking to the archetypal modern man on the assembly line, it overlooks that majority of the population who are immature, retired, invalided, unemployed, or working as housewives. Rather few of them have the blessed simplicity of a time clock that tells them when they are supposed to be in a state of work and when at leisure. Of course, the dichotomy contains an important measure of truth, but "work" probably is not as useful a term for it as is the colloquial notion of a "job." That is, some sort of task mandate, some position in the social sun, continues to define our station in life and continues to be one of life's major enjoyments. At any rate for Americans retirement and unemployment prove to be more devastating for mental than for material reasons. Lacking a job, one is likely to drift, inwardly as well as outwardly. Most people do have some sort of job, even if it is not on an assembly line. Any such prolonged expenditure of effort—even of effort so enjoyable as writing a book—takes its toll in foregone alternatives. To the extent that this is so, nearly all of us recognize after hours during which we search for enjoyments that will help restore a sense of "completeness" and well-being.

The Approach

I take it as my job in these pages to offer an interpretive report. It is too soon to comb the Japanese after hours with fine-toothed theory; I prefer to depict the Japanese scene in such a way that it will be useful as a cultural opposing self. In doing so I pay homage to those who have strived to help the West understand the Japanese encounter with modernity, from Basil Hall Chamberlain and Lafcadio Hearn in the nineteenth century to scholars in many fields today. I also recognize what I owe to my mentors. And though I have borrowed ideas from many of them, I have been overwhelmingly influenced by the cultural anthropology of Clyde Kluckhohn, the social psychology of David Riesman, and the insights into Japanese life imparted to me by John Pelzel.

By training I am an ethnographer, by temperament an eclectic. Both traits have influenced my methods of study and my selections of data. As an ethnographer I am partial to direct participation in—and observation of —ongoing human activities. I am, to use Milton Singer's phrasing, less attracted to the study of "texts" than to the study of "contexts." And although at times I write of modern Japan as a whole, the bulk of what I say applies primarily to a region in Honshu Island where I lived and studied in 1959 and 1960. As an eclectic I prefer to draw from many sources. So in addition to field materials the reader will encounter selections from opinion surveys, scholarly monographs, weekly magazines, the minutes of a young wives' club, and even from newspaper clippings that were collected for me by a Tokyo news service. After all, although fieldwork is the ethnographer's time-honored way of gaining information (and some types of information can be obtained in no other way), it has obvious limits in the study of modern civilizations. What is typical of one community need not be typical of the region; what is typical of the region may be atypical for the nation. But on the other hand, to flee into the sociologist's sanctuary, the "stratified random sample," is to miss the richness of the ongoing scene. I know of no formula that guarantees that one can escape these extremes. One has to play by ear, and I claim to have done no more.

Then there is the problem of great versus little traditions. For in a society where all are workers and all are aristocrats it becomes difficult to sort out what is capital-letter Culture from what is commonplace, lower-case culture. "Popular culture" is not always lowbrow; "vernacular culture" is participated in by all persons, to some extent. Here I lean toward the lower case. The reader seeking materials on the classical Japanese great tradition will be disappointed. I think it true that this great tradition is virtually unstudied *as a mode of social relations*, even though its art forms and philosophical postulates have long been under scrutiny. But, because of time and resources (and perhaps because of personal predilections), I did not attempt such an investigation. I am also convinced that the more commonplace affairs of Japanese life continue to be seriously underreported in the West, despite the interest in Japan shown by the media of mass communications.

I have tried to be selective and apposite. In this I have followed the advice of Chamberlain, introducing his delightful little dictionary of *Things Japanese:* "The old and the new will be found cheek by jowl. What will not be found is padding; for padding is unpardonable in any book on Japan, where the material is so plentiful that the chief difficulty is to know what to omit." I am writing mostly for the nonspecialist. I expect that my reader may have been to Japan; surely knows people who have; and at the very least has a few notions about the land and its people. But I expect no familiarity with the Japanese language, and wherever possible I have translated from Japanese sources, out of a feeling that even poor translations will convey some Japanese flavor. The original sources are cited in Notes (p. 197 ff.), which also suggest further readings. Japanese personal names are given according to Japanese usage: first the patronym, then the individual name. To further the flavor of Japaneseness I have eschewed the usual photographs of sullen natives scowling at the ethnographer's camera, in favor of drawings by Mr. Yanagisawa Takeshi. A few remarks on Mr. Yanagisawa and the illustrations are given in the Notes.

I also have tried to compensate for my feelings, such as I know them. Not to hide them; rather to prevent them from becoming obtrusive. Having struggled to understand the Japanese I find myself sympathetically involved with them. At the same time, as a native American I find myself annoyed by such of their traits and tendencies as run across the grain of my Illinois upbringing. And romantic stirrings at times prompt me to idolize the Japan of the Tokugawa period (1603–1868) at the expense of the Japan of today. I cannot claim the deep-rooted feeling for things Japanese which is the native's by birthright. But I do believe that years of study and participation have made it possible for me to escape many of the genuine, but misleading, impressions which fog the casual traveler's vision. My Japanese friends will tell me where I have erred, and so for that matter may my Western readers. For both can see what I cannot—the self and the face behind these words.

2. Under the Eaves

Ine no kake
toriharawarete
harewataru
tō ne ni yuki no
miyuru konogoro.

TAIBI

As the rice-racks
are stored away,
and the sky clears off,
on the far peaks
see the snow these days!

The Roof of Japan

The mountains that girdle the center of Honshu Island are sometimes still called the Hida Range. But the average Japanese today knows them only by the East-West binomial *Nihon Arupusu*, the Japan Alps. The term is credited to the British missionary Walter Weston, although others seem to have used it before he did. Weston tramped the range for two decades, over the turn of the century, and devoted two books to his journeys. In recent years grateful innkeepers and tourist bureaus have enshrined the Reverend Weston in a plaque at Kamikōchi, where they annually stage a festival to preserve his memory.

The Northern Range of the Alps reaches directly southward from the Japan Sea for nearly a hundred miles. It has some forty peaks above 8,000 feet, snow-clad half the year and more. East of the range for its southernmost forty miles at a 1,600-foot elevation is the basin of the Anchiku region. The basin is narrow and tear-drop shaped, ten to fifteen miles wide at its southern end, tapering gradually to the north. Today it is home to 400,000 Japanese, who earn their livelihood from fruit and cereal crops and from a panoply of light industries and services.

The Alps dominate the basin. They set the tenor of its life today, much as in the past. Rugged masters, they keep a jealous company. Most of the time they give ample water for the paddies and for hydroelectric power. But sometimes they catch typhoon-borne rains and dump them onto the plain in flash floods. In a few hours these debris-choked torrents can spoil acres of paddy and wipe away years of patient work on dikes and bridges. Riverbeds in the plain are as much as a half mile wide, dry and stony most of the year, useful only to gravel diggers.

In earlier generations the people of the plain looked to the Alps for timber and game. But since Weston's time Anchiku people have increasingly been looking to the mountains as the source of an even more lucrative and perhaps less expendable revenue animal, the vacationer. In winter there are skiing and skating, in summer hiking, climbing, camping. In all seasons the hot springs resorts that rim the basin are open. Diesel express trains bring the region within easy weekending distance both from the Tokyo-Yokohama megalopolis to the east and from Nagoya to the south. A scenic highway is being bulldozed into the Alps from the center of the basin. And there has been talk of opening a helicopter sightseeing service to some of the peaks.

Vacationing is not new to Anchiku, although its forms have changed with the changing times. The region has always been a hinterland, but at the same time always closely linked with the central cities since the founding of the Japanese state in the sixth century A.D. For a while in the eighth century the basin harbored the capitol of Shinano province (approximately present-day Nagano Prefecture). In the eyes of Kyoto courtiers the region must have appeared as a kind of exotic but safe tramontane. Here one could escape the pressures of the capitol, enjoy the alpine prospect, bathe in the hot springs, and yet not be too near the barbarous tribes on the northern frontier. One of the first times the region is mentioned in court records is under an entry for 710 when the Temmu emperor sent retainers to Yamabe Springs on the east side of the valley. The emperor, apparently unwell, planned to recuperate there but died en route. Generations of poets have left their tributes to the scenery, and the "blue blue skies of Shinano" have long been in the repertoire of classical allusion.

As the discerning eye can read from a man's face the outlines of his history, so it can read from the face of a land the outlines of its becoming. Prehistoric settlers in Anchiku seem to have clung to the uplands; the lower basin presumably was uninhabitable marshland. At any rate, although Anchiku is rich in artifacts from all major periods in Japanese prehistory, most of these have been recovered from the slopes and from hillside caves. By the early centuries of our era, settlers were moving down the alluvial fans and onto the valley floor itself. Place names suggest this, and so do the dozens of burial mounds characteristic of the protohistoric period (often called the Tomb period) which dot the entire basin.

Men of early historic times (seventh to twelfth centuries) wrote their passing on the land in several ways. They cut roads along the foot of the hills, and many of these roads still are used. Every few miles they built forts to defend these roads, and the remains of many of these forts are easy to find. They built temples along the roads, and a few of these have escaped not only time but the ravages of a temple-burning fever that fell upon Anchiku in the anti-Buddhist years after 1868. They organized a circuit of traveling fairs, and the names of some of these periodic marketplaces survive as hamlet names today (e.g., *Tōkaichi*, "tenth-day market").

The feudal period (thirteenth to sixteenth centuries) saw the raising of more formidable fortifications, including the beginnings of the castle town of Matsumoto. Although sovereignty changed hands several times,

Anchiku was peaceful until the middle of the sixteenth century. In the decade of the 1550's the forces of Takeda Shingen marched in from the southeast, from Kai (now Yamanashi Prefecture). They destroyed Anchiku's forts, and they slew or drove off many of its people. (Even the oldest families in the basin today cannot trace their ancestry beyond this period.) Driven from their domain, the Ogasawara lord and his household allied themselves with the up-and-coming Tokugawa Ieyasu. With his aid they were able to retake Matsumoto in 1582. And in 1585 Ogasawara Sadayoshi ordered the building of the castle whose keep and moats still form the nucleus of Matsumoto City.

Anchiku was a microcosm of Japanese development in the Tokugawa era (1600–1868). Except for a famine in the 1830's, it prospered. Except for a peasant uprising in 1686 (twenty leaders were tried and slain), it was pacific. The Matsumoto lords adopted the general Tokugawa administrative plan: samurai were ordered to live at the foot of the castle, all other persons were forbidden to bear arms. Households were organized into mutual surveillance groups. Christianity was outlawed, and detailed sumptuary edicts were issued. District administrative offices were established at several points linked by a network of roads. These roads no longer hugged the hills but struck directly across the valley floor with only minor concessions to terrain. Posthouses and milestones were erected at regular intervals (a few can be seen today). Commerce with neighboring domains grew steadily, and the castle soon was surrounded by large merchant quarters. In the middle of the eighteenth century the townsmen class was only a fraction more numerous than the samurai class. By the end of the era it outnumbered the samurai twofold.

After 1868 Anchiku swiftly joined the world of modernity. But to see these changes we must move closer. Let us look first at Matsumoto, then at a rural community.

The Social Summit

As the Alps dominate the basin geographically, so Matsumoto City dominates it socially. Though geographically on the eastern fringe, politically Matsumoto was the center of the region by the eighth century, and the passage of time did little to dim its importance. Indeed its importance has risen along with the trend toward urban-industrial concentration that marks Japan's modern century. From 1860 to 1960 its population increased more than fivefold. This is well above the general national increase (threefold), although well below the increase in the great metropolises such as Tokyo (tenfold). Today Matsumoto is an urban sprawl with some 80,000 residents. In census reports it is credited with 150,000, but nearly half of these live in former rural communities amalgamated under the city administration in the late 1950's.

The traveler who detrains in Matsumoto today without benefit of a city map is likely to be consumed by one emotion: bewilderment. He encounters a railway station that is sizable but undistinguished. Second story windows afford him only a limited view consisting of the station plaza, a fan of streets, and fragments of the city's upper architecture. He sees a plaza that is a collage of paving brick, billboards, and power poles. Buses in red-yellow-blue uniforms are at right dress across the front of it. Taxis in various hues scoot around them with civilian casualness. A trolley car of 1920 vintage makes incredible rumbles as it threads around the plaza and shuffles off down the center of the one wide street.

Across the plaza the traveler sees a community of bus stops, restaurants, coffee houses, newsstands, souvenir shops, and advertisements for hot springs. Beyond, he can discern only a few structures that draw attention by rising above the general rooftop level. In all directions, but especially to south and west, he sees thickets of factory and bathhouse chimneys. To the north on the distant upslope are bright rows of concrete apartments and the blue-white monolith of the university hospital. Nearer to the eye are the upper floors of department stores. In the middle distance he can glimpse a part of the new city hall, and the peak of the Ogasawara castle keep. And atop the hills east of the city he can make out the transmitting poles of two television stations.

If he is an ethnographer the traveler is likely to wonder whether any of these would qualify as the city's master institution—whether any of these structures would provide him with a masterkey to understanding what really matters most in Matsumoto's world, the sun around which all other institutions are planetary. And if he is a conscientious ethnographer he will stop to record an impression that modern Matsumoto is as pluralistic as modern Madison, Wisconsin, and that a whole handful of institutions are contending for priority.

This was not true of Matsumoto in the Tokugawa period. Then it had, like most Japanese castle towns of its day, a symmetry that was, however fearful, easily framed by mortal eye. One cannot always read directly from the lines of a town plan the lines of its social order, yet the two rarely seem far divergent. And perhaps the quickest way to understand how Matsumoto has been transformed by modernity is to see how its castle-town plan came by turns to be accommodated, outgrown, and finally rejected.

The earlier Matsumoto had an unmistakable single center and source of being. This was the fiefdom castle, with a five-story keep that overlooked the entire town but was cushioned from its vulgar incursions by a triple series of moats. Between the moats nearest the castle lived the samurai and their families; farther out, the lesser footmen and retainers. Streets were oriented to the cardinal points of the compass and were spaced at regular intervals. Within the walls they were wider than without, and they were lined with more imposing houses.

The only major threat, and that a relatively disorganized one, came from the hustle and color of the merchant quarters. With the improved roads of the eighteenth century, brokerage trade began to centralize in Matsumoto. A brisk trade developed particularly between Matsumoto and Nagoya. Matsumoto brokers bought up Anchiku hemp, paper, tobacco, and medicinal herbs and dispatched them to Nagoya. Nagoya brokers repaid with pottery, hardware, tea, salt, and dried fish. One guide for travelers to Zenkōji—a nationally popular pilgrimage center in Nagano City—remarks that Matsumoto daily dispatched a thousand loaded pack horses and took delivery of another thousand.

The main road approached the castle directly from the south but was turned away at the outer moat. It passed around the castle to the east, then continued north on its way to Zenkōji. Lesser roads radiated into all parts of the basin. Shops and inns lined these roads, and the majority of Matsumoto's retail stores today are in the same locations. Store fronts were low and narrow and plain, in accord with sumptuary regulations. But one suspects that in their inner quarters and gardens, hidden from the street, wealthier merchants indulged in splendor with relative impunity. In the townsmen's quarters were the theaters and pleasure houses, and it is likely that more than one samurai crossed the moats in disguise, bent on sampling forbidden fruits.

Temples and shrines were, generally speaking, on the edges of the town, as though to ward off hopefully the elements, or in any case the rustics beyond.

Along with the rest of the nation, Matsumoto saw many changes in the first dozen years after the Meiji restoration. But seen against the town plan these changes seem to be less revolutionary than evolutionary, matters of descent with modifications. The fiefdom administration was renamed a prefectural administration and continued much as before. Then in 1871 Matsumoto became the capital of newly created Chikuma Prefecture, an amalgam of Anchiku with several neighboring fiefs. But when the administrative offices were gutted by fire in 1876 the former fiefs were parceled out, and Anchiku has since then been a part of Nagano Prefecture. All this had relatively little direct effect upon the face of the town, but there were other marks of the newborn nation. A post office was opened, and soon telegraph wires were strung from Nagano City. There was a district court, a newspaper company, and a branch of the national bank. Silk and cocoon brokerages began to appear in numbers as overseas markets opened. Christian missionaries were seen in the streets. And a primary school of Western style—copied from a building in Tokyo which had been copied from a school in Boston—was erected, replete with a Victorian turret, just outside the south castle gate.

Only in the third Meiji decade did the inroads of industrial technology begin to sketch the shape of a new kind of city. A net of electric wires was thrown across the city in 1899, and was joined a decade later by another of telephone lines. What official reports called "workshops with machines" sprung up in all parts of town. And in 1901 on the southeastern edge of town the Katakura Corporation opened a vast modern spinning mill—an industrial castle whose size and pretensions began to rival those of the old political castle. Soon there were still other contenders. Railway lines came through from Nagano City and Tokyo in 1902; and from Nagoya in 1911; a branch was built up the center of the valley to Ōmachi in 1916. The Matsumoto terminal was located a half mile southwest of the castle and off from the major shopping streets. Expectably enough, commerce and industry began to move in its direction. And at the same time the railway made it possible for people in many parts of Anchiku to commute to the new factories and to the new higher schools being opened during these years. By the end of the Meiji era the castle had lost its hegemony. In sheer height and architectural harmony perhaps it still outclassed any other Matsumoto structure. But commerce, industry, education, and transportation all were moving in other directions.

The Taisho period (1912–1925) was a time of prosperity, on the whole, and a time when the new classes of white and blue collar workers developed a modern style of city living. Water and gas mains were laid throughout Matsumoto. Concrete and stucco façades began to replace the drab, recessed fronts of the nineteenth-century shops. Vaudeville halls were converted to movie theaters. Suburban housing tracts were opened.

22

A trolley line was run to Asama Springs, on the north-eastern edge of town, and another line straight across the valley to where the Atsusa River emerges from the Alps. Vacationers from the coastal cities began to be seen in large numbers, and near the station plaza there grew a new town of hotels and restaurants. And motor-buses and trucks brought almost every corner of Anchiku within a half day's travel.

Good years continued through the 1920's and into the 1930's. The prefectural government built an impressive athletic ground on the northern upslope, and the national government created a vast public park up in the Alps. But the worldwide depression of the 'thirties slowed development to a crawl and sent the silk market into a tailspin. The growth of militarism in the nation was reflected in Matsumoto in the building of an army barracks and, later, of military factories. Thought control and indoctrination were fostered not only in the schools but also in the form of a "public hall"—built next to a monument commemorating the Meiji emperor's visit to the city—with its affiliated youth clubs and neighborhood watch-and-ward societies.

The United States Army Air Forces apparently did not regard Matsumoto as a major target during the war. This is not entirely a blessing, for a number of the bombed-out cities have been rebuilt with wide boulevards capable of bearing mass motor traffic. Matsumoto finds itself caught in a web of streets designed for pedestrians and pack horses. Traffic is bumper-to-bumper on most main thoroughfares during much of the day. A bypass highway is being built to siphon off the worst of the through traffic; but herculean efforts within the city have so far sufficed only to widen part of one main street.

In the early postwar years there was a severe housing shortage, made worse by a heavy influx of returnees from the former colonies. Government-sponsored apartment projects and housing tracts by the dozen have been opened all around the city, increasing its areal sprawl by perhaps as much as a third. Under Occupation influence, the militarist indoctrination and surveillance groups were abolished. The "public hall" (*kōkaidō*) was renamed "people's hall" (*kōminkan*), its mat flooring was replaced with chairs, and it was given the task of adult education and the spreading of democratic ideals. The lower schools were converted to a 6-3-3 American-style system, and several new buildings were erected. When the new prefectural university was organized in 1949, three of its colleges were awarded to Matsumoto. The school of education and the schools of law and literature took over the campus of the prewar national high school. The school of medicine fell heir to the army barracks.

With the rising prosperity of the decade, new buildings are rising throughout Matsumoto: supermarkets, department stores, hotels, factories, apartments. There is an imposing city auditorium on the south side and a seven-story city hall on the east rim of the second moat, overshadowing the five-story castle. Sadayoshi's former stronghold is now preserved as an official national treasure, and its grounds are a public park. His town plan now is Matsumoto's sorrow, but at least his castle serves as a tourist attraction. It was rebuilt in the early fifties when it showed signs of tumbling. A new gatehouse was added (copied from one in Nagoya) in 1960. And in 1959 there was a fillip to its history as it momentarily became the site of a national scandal. A newspaper reporter discovered that a group of local politicians, apparently bored with meeting at their usual run of Matsumoto and Asama inns, had persuaded the caretaker to look the other way while they invaded the castle for an evening of boozing fellowship.

The Vanishing Village

Fifteen miles up the valley from Matsumoto is a station stop called Ariake. From the station a gravel-topped prefectural highway angles west across the Nakabusa River and into the foothills. It threads through the former Ariake village, winds around the south slopes of the conical peak of the same name ("Shinano's Mount Fuji") and ends at a small hot spring. From late June until September the road is under a cloud of dust, as an almost endless procession of taxis and buses carries vacationers from the station to the hot spring, which also is a gateway for Alpine hiking. Weston, having had reports of "an enchanted valley penetrating into the recesses of the main chain of the Northern Alps," passed this way by rickshaw and on foot in August, 1912. He pronounced the Nakabusa Valley "of surpassing loveliness, each turn of the winding glen more romantic than the last," and praised the hot spring and local hospitality. His one complaint was against "the boorish behavior of some lads of the rougher student class" whose offense seems to have been that they enjoyed singing in the baths late at night. "In this respect," added Weston, "they differ seriously from those ancient Greeks whom in so many ways they otherwise resemble, for the Athenians considered noisy singing in public baths a special sign of boorishness."

The rest of the year, traffic on the prefectural highway is much lighter. However, there continue to be morning and evening rushes of bikes and motorbikes ridden by Ariake residents who commute to schools, offices, and workshops in several basin towns. Rush hour is as much a part of the present-day Anchiku rural scene as are its acres upon acres of ripening rice and mulberry. Mechanization and improved crop techniques have made the Anchiku farmer as much a technical specialist as his American counterpart—and rice yields per acre have nearly doubled since the war. Urbanization and industrialization have opened a Pandora's box of new occupations—and all major basin towns are within an hour and a half's travel. Most Ariake residents will tell you they are farmers. But less than a quarter of them make their livelihood solely from farming, and the combinations of farming with different kinds of wage work are so varied as to defy generalization. The typical holding can adequately be worked by one or two able-bodied adults. Outside help is needed only during the critical spring days when rice is transplanted from seed beds to main fields. Children are expected to devote their time to their schoolwork. It is perhaps most common for the head of a household to manage the farm, with his wife's assistance. Adult sons and daughters will take up work in the towns. Nevertheless it is not unusual for household heads also to find other employment, especially during the winter months (the Anchiku growing season is 150 days). And if he can secure a permanent position in town, the household head may delegate day-to-day farm tasks to his wife while he commutes to work and helps in the fields on his days off.

In short, Ariake has an urban hustle that belies its rural vistas. There are still arcadian touches, but it is a noisy arcadia most of the year. The dawn comes up as on an infantry skirmish, with automatic scarecrows (carbide guns) booming on all sides. During the daytime, heavy traffic rumbles along the prefectural highway, motor tricycles bounce on the byways, power cultivators sputter from the paddies, and radios blare from the farmyards. In the evening cool, public address systems from half a dozen directions compete for attention as they broadcast popular music and advertise the night's meetings at their respective hamlet people's halls.

The district cuts an irregular swath about four miles wide, from the center of the valley to the top of the Alps. It is bounded on the west by the Alpine divide; on the other three sides by the Karasu and Nakabusa rivers. The western two-thirds of the district is mountainous national park and forest, inhabited only during the summer months. Permanent residents are all situated in the eastern third, in the valley. The lower half of the valley section slants very gently eastward but the upper half is a steep and stony alluvium. In some places there are stone fences reminiscent of New England. Most of the soil is porous granitic sand. To develop good paddy, the farmer must often carry in less porous topsoils, sometimes from a considerable distance. One folk explanation for the place name is that the sandy paths reflect brightly on moonlit nights (*ariake*, literally "having light," but also "daybreak"). However this does not account for Mount Ariake, which was named long ago, and from which the village took its name in the nineteenth century. Even today about half the cultivated area is given over to dry-field crops such as wheat, beans, mulberry, and vegetables. However, irrigation water is abundant in most parts of the district; with the silk market continuing to decline, Ariake farmers have been rapidly converting dry fields to paddy.

Matsumoto's modern history has been one of continuing diversification; Ariake's has been one first of centralization then of gradual dispersion. For eighty years Ariake was a corporate village. In 1874 administrative convenience created it out of seven Tokugawa hamlets; in 1955 administrative convenience reduced it to being a district of Hotaka Town.

In the Tokugawa period the district contained seven hamlets, with an estimated total population of two thousand persons. Each hamlet had a fair degree of self-sufficiency, although it marketed some cash crops through the Matsumoto brokerage channels. It had also a fair degree of self-government, reinforced by control over communal lands and woods, although it was answerable to the Matsumoto lord for failure to keep the peace or forward annual taxes. One hamlet was under the Hotaka magistrate to the south, the others under the Matsukawa magistrate to the north.

Meiji leaders held a conscious policy of coaxing loyalties away from the hamlets onto the newly created administrative villages. First, they put local administration and record keeping into the hands of an elected mayor and council. Hamlet boundaries were redrawn by administrative decision; and although the hamlets retained some functions (and, until 1946, their common lands), their officers tended to become unpaid assistants to the village council. Second, a village-wide tutelary shrine was established, and by definition all residents became its supporters. Third, public primary schools were organized at the village level, in the correct (for Japan) expectation that those who had attended the same school would later find hamlet loyalties heavily counterbalanced by loyalties to village-wide classmates. Applied to Ariake, these policies had by the turn of the century resulted in a new cluster of buildings near the center of the valley section of the village—a primary school, post office, village office, fire station, and a handful of stores. In the twentieth century this has become the commercial center of the village. Its nearest rivals are all across the river and along the railway. Today it has more than two dozen stores and workshops, a police box, producers' coöperative, dentist's office, and forestry field office all strung out along the prefectural highway and a cross-road. And it still is known as Schoolville (*Gakkō-machi*), although the school was torn down in the late 1940's and a larger one built a mile up the road. The village tutelary is still further distant, in the foothills near where the Nakabusa debouches onto the plain.

Villagers in the Tokugawa period were by no means immune from the lure of the cities. But after the turn of the century modern transportation and telecommunications began to bring the city close to hand, and the newly developed village loyalties began to disappear. In Ariake the favored few who were able to attend the higher schools in Matsumoto in the Meiji era were obliged to live in the city. There were horsedrawn stages, but the trip consumed more than three hours. However, commuting began to be possible after the railway was built during the First World War, and in 1925 bus service began between Schoolville and the station. Then, too, factories were rising not only in Matsumoto but closer at hand in Toyoshina, Hotaka, and Ōmachi. And in the early 'twenties the Washinton (i.e., "Washington") Corporation built a shoe factory in the southeast corner of the village and began to employ some 150 hands. Village electrification began after 1911, when a hydroelectric generating plant was erected in the foothills along the Nakabusa River. And the post office installed a switchboard and forty telephones in 1919. Unused land, however stony, was still available; and the silk market continued to climb. By 1925 Ariake's population had grown to double what it had been a century earlier, during a period when Japan's rural population in general was at a standstill.

In the slump years of the 1930's the Ariake population leveled at slightly below its 1925 peak. A small artillery training camp was opened along the Karasu River; and the government fostered public halls and youth groups and producers' coöperatives here as elsewhere. One ambitious landlord attempted to stimulate the production of shantung, but with middling results.

Since the war, changes have been many and continuous. Immediately after the war the official population was swelled more than a thousand by evacuees from the bombed cities and by returnees from the former colonies. Paupers camped in the dry riverbeds. However, as economic conditions improved, the bulk of the returnees went elsewhere. By 1960 the population had dropped back to slightly above the 1925 peak.

From 1946 to 1950 the village was in the turmoil of the land reform program. Landlordism had not been so severe an issue in Ariake as in many villages. Less than ten per cent of the arable land in the village in 1946 was owned by absentee landlords; and only two landlords, both resident, had holdings of more than twenty acres. Nevertheless some 710 acres changed hands during the reforms. In 1946 only 27 per cent of Ariake farmers were independent (i.e. nonrenting); by 1950 the proportion had increased to 70 per cent.

Here as elsewhere in Japan the reforms seem on the

whole to have genuinely spurred productivity. The trend has been further encouraged by the (now independent) producers' coöperatives, which have energetically urged rational crop management and diversification. Many Ariake families have begun to raise poultry and pigs and sheep for sale, and a few have begun to experiment with beef cattle and milch cows. One Nagoya dairy has put up milk collection sheds along the prefectural highway.

In 1946 one part of the artillery ground was opened as a development project for returnees. And in 1958 the Agriculture and Forestry Bureau sent in bulldozers and planners, and began a model reclamation project using the remainder of the old camp. Paddies were laid out in neat rectangular blocks large enough for efficient use of power cultivators. Concrete irrigation canals were installed. And communal tool sheds were provided, so that families entering the project moved into city-style houses, complete with tile kitchens and running water. At the same time, the rest of Ariake banded together to sink a well and lay pipes that would bring running water to the older houses in the district too. In 1949 the central government established a boys' reform school on the edge of the foothills, taking over a building that had been used as a private school during the war, and before that as a resort. "The hill where the bell sounds," a radio drama about the boys' school, in the mid-1950's brought a moment of nationwide attention, which Ariake people still vividly remember.

Postwar administrators have been dealing with the villages much as their grandfathers did with the hamlets. Loyalties and administrative functions are being shifted to larger amalgamated townships, much as in the West. The Ariake administration was abolished in

1955; and, apart from tax registers, all Ariake records are now compiled by the Hotaka town office. Similarly the (now compulsory) middle school is a town-wide middle school, although Ariake does retain its primary school. However, Meiji and postwar policies diverge on one point: the postwar leaders have left untouched the shrines, which now are constitutionally separate from the state.

Schoolville today has neither school nor village administration, but it continues to grow commercially. There is a new post office and fire station, and several new shops: druggist, watchmaker, gasoline station. And the producers' coöperative has begun to invade the old village office for use as a meeting hall.

3. *New Forms, New*
Turns, New Terms

In modern civilization the making of new forms of man takes new turns, which may demand new terms for their description.

ROBERT REDFIELD

33

The scene set, we call in performers. We introduce three ways of living in modern Anchiku.

People guide themselves by ideologies and utopias, they do not ordinarily "live" them. They live most immediately within a landscape of everyday constraints and possibilities. Within these they evolve a more or less orderly, more or less meaningful, more or less satisfying way of life. The landscape is dominated by daily work and by family ties. One need not be a philosophical materialist in order to recognize the extent to which (borrowing the words of Joseph Schumpeter) "it is our daily work which forms our minds, and that it is our location within the productive process which determines our outlook on things—or the sides of things we see— and the social elbowroom at the command of each of us." Likewise one need not be a family sociologist to recognize the extent to which we are checked and at the same time balanced by those with whom we daily eat, sleep, and commune. So we must speak not only of the new forms of "man" in modern civilization but also of the new forms of family living. We might call them family cultures or subcultures. But since we are going to deal with the over-all manner or mode, it will be simplest to speak of family styles.

The term style calls our attention to format rather than substance. It directs us to the manner of singing rather than the song. It asks us to look for motifs, to see them bound together in related sets, and to recognize how the resulting effect is colored by general qualities.

Three stylistic traditions of family living stand out in Japan's recent centuries. They are those of the managers, the countrymen, and the merchants. Other traditions are visible but not numerically preponderant: examples are those of the artist and intellectual, the pariah, the laborer, or the elite. Behind the modern manifestations of each of these styles one can readily find Tokugawa roots (scratch a salaryman, find a samurai). Indeed we must never lose sight of these. What follows is not meant as a history of these styles, but it is meant as an indication of continuity within change. All of them are new men, but all of them have a traditional side as well.

The Salaryman

The salaryman, the Japanese version of white-collar worker, is a samurai reincarnate. A knight of modern capitalism, he resembles the Tokugawa knight official on many points. Simple comparisons tend to overstate the case, but the points of similarity and difference are worth attending.

Samurai and salaryman alike profess long-term allegiance to an establishment, and both receive in return long-term job security with a dependable, periodic stipend. Both commute daily to the office; both have fixed hours of labor and fixed holidays. Both are implicated in factional disputes among their peers and seniors in the establishment. Each is the cynosure of his social order. And both reside in "choice" locations.

There are also important differences. The salaryman is, as the samurai was not, equal before the law with his fellowmen: he wears no swords. Samurai were officials; some salarymen are too, but many more are employed in commercial corporations. The samurai ordinarily inherited his status; the salaryman must achieve his, proving his fitness by earning a college degree and passing the company's entrance examination.

Historically, too, the tie is close. After 1868 the first

generation of modern bureaucrats and industrial managers had to be recruited, not surprisingly, for the most part from disestablished samurai. This changeover from topknot to top hat (which should not be overstressed, for many samurai had been employed in managerial tasks) is expressive of the government-led tenor of Japan's early modernization. But by the turn of the twentieth century the retread samurai was beginning to step aside for a new form of man, a "Voltairean Japanese," as Chamberlain called him at the time, the product of the modern university. The new man won himself a new term, a term created in Japanized English, *sarariiman.*

As Japanese industry and bureaucracy have grown during the past half century, so have their "knowledge workers," the salarymen. Today the salaryman makes up perhaps as much as a fifth of the Japanese labor force— although an exact count is impossible. His style of life is a target of nationwide envy and youthful ambition, and it is widely imitated. In the Tokugawa period the "Five Breaks" (*go sekku*), five annual holidays favored by the samurai, grew popular among townsmen and peasants. In the modern era the Weekly Holiday System, which rapidly became part of the salaryman style, is copied by merchants and even by farmers. Apprentices and salesgirls now demand a six-day or five-and-one-half day working week. And perhaps most telling of all is the instituting—at places in Anchiku as elsewhere—of what is called a "farmers' salary system." Under this system, the farmer takes the bulk of his income from annual crop sales and deposits it with the treasurer of the local producers' coöperative. The treasurer repays the money in monthly installments, as a "salary." Advocates say that the system encourages thrift, and monthly budgeting, and of course it provides the coöperative with added short-term working capital. One Ariake farmer was oversimple in his social arithmetic but perhaps accurate in his emotional arithmetic when he remarked to me, "These days half of the Japanese are salarymen, and the other half are trying to live as if they were."

There are abundant parallels with the American scene. Indeed, in reading Japanese commentaries on the salaryman one often suspects that C. Wright Mills is being quoted without credit. Certainly many phrases may be taken from *White Collar* and applied directly to the salaryman: his Kafka-like alienation from his work, his felt disjunction of effort and enjoyment, his political voicelessness, his need to sell not only his labor but also his personality, and so on. The salaryman is a key figure for understanding the modern social configuration. As Mills writes, "By their rise to numerical importance, the white-collar people have upset the nineteenth-century expectation that society would be divided between entrepreneurs and wage workers. By their mass way of life, they have transformed the tang and feel of the American experience. They carry, in a most revealing way, many of those psychological themes that characterize our epoch, and, in one way or another, every general theory of the main drift has had to take account of them."

The Firm Framework

When the salaryman's style of living is viewed in contrast to those of the farmer and the merchant, these features stand out: Of the three the salaryman is financially the most stable but, at the same time, the least independent. The establishment shelters him against any major income fluctuations—up as well as down, however—but demands of him what is often called a "lifetime commitment." Taken naïvely, the phrase is hyperbolic; twenty-five-year men are not difficult to uncover in American bureaus and corporations too. However, it does call attention to a discernible sluggishness in salaryman mobility from employer to employer, a prizing of company loyalty, and a reluctance to hire a man who has once been another's knight or squire. To this extent the salaryman has much less room in which to maneuver than do the merchant and the farmer, however much the latter two might prefer not to liquidate their enterprises.

The salaryman's life is more clearly segregated into a workshop sphere and a household sphere. Although he may carry his office problems home with him, his wife and children do not ordinarily enter into his office activities except as spurs to his ambitions. Here again he has less maneuverability than the farmer or merchant, who are in a better position to exploit the labor power of other family members. Salaryman wives often take jobs during the early years of marriage. But, once children are in the household, the place of the proper salaryman wife, like that of the proper samurai wife, is in the home.

With his life so dependent upon the social framework of his office, the salaryman, more than the farmer or merchant, must learn to exploit his personality. True enough, the merchant sells his friendliness and service as well as his goods. But the salaryman has little in the way of objective goods to offer; he must sell his subjective self, and in an all but monopsonistic market. He needs to be almost diseasedly sensitive to his relationships with peers and seniors. In this regard he is, if anything, more trapped in the social framework than even the stereotypic farmer in the stereotypic village.

The social framework also weighs heavily upon the salaryman's patterns of work and play. Ideally his hours can be divided into worktime and playtime with an ease unknown to the farmer or the merchant. But in practice the dividing line grows dim. On demand from the establishment the salaryman is expected to relinquish his playtime freely and without carping, and to perform overtime tasks or take on special assignments. Again, it is a common salaryman practice not to absent himself for the full period of his regular vacation, lest doubts be raised about his loyalty. Furthermore, after-hours socializing with his office mates might not seem to be a part of his job description; but it is so much a part of what is routinely expected of him that if he persistently fails to join in the "fun" he risks serious sanctions.

Finally, the salaryman cannot ordinarily expect to pass on his position to his child, as the farmer or merchant may. If his children are to succeed in life, they will need the best schooling possible. And anxiety over their scholastic merit is a daily household companion for salaryman families. Such anxiety is of course not absent from the homes of farmers and merchants; they too wish to see their children rise in the world. But for the salaryman the issue is especially acute.

Hikari ga Oka

In old Matsumoto, as in the typical Tokugawa castle town, samurai residences circled the castle, hard by the innermost moats. For its day this was the most desirable neighborhood, second only to that of the lord himself, with wider streets, higher gates, more imposing gardens than those permitted the townsmen living beyond the outer moats. Today the old samurai quarters are filled with offices, hospitals, inns, restaurants, and shops. And now most salarymen live on the suburban fringes, in single-family dwellings, in company tracts, and in modern apartment projects.

The Hikari ga Oka apartments are on the lower slopes of a hillside overlooking the city. The project was opened in 1959 with 154 units in a dozen brightly painted steel-and-concrete structures of two or three floors. It was financed by the prefectural government, and it is provided for the platoons of salarymen who staff the Matsumoto administrative offices, telecommunications service, public hospitals, and schools. The apartments are not spacious even by Japanese standards, but they are new and cheery and they rent for half of what comparable space would cost elsewhere in town. Each dwelling unit has two mat-floored rooms, one of six mats and one of four and a half. (A mat is approximately three by six feet). It also has a nine by nine foot wood-floored kitchen, a toilet, and a small entryway. Some units have a veranda and a bath (other residents must use a public bathhouse) but are otherwise identical. Units with bath and veranda rent for 2,700 yen a month; others for 1,700 yen.

Seen from outside, the project looks very much like apartment projects in the West, with two exceptions. There are no rows of parked cars, and there is but one telephone line. The only phone for 154 households is a pay unit in a booth on the corner of the project playground.

Most husbands and wives in Hikari ga Oka are in their thirties or early forties. Nearly every family has a child or two at the preschool or primary school stage; and a few have managed to squeeze in a grandmother or a husband's sibling. Most families complain of crowding and are putting money aside in hopes of building or buying a private residence in a few years. They regard the project as a way station, comfortable enough for all that but not permanent. They hesitate to firm up their local ties: for example, they have voted down an invitation to become official supporters of the neighborhood shrine, although some families contribute privately to its upkeep.

Torii Gekkyū

One of the first-floor units in block G—the blocks are identified by roman letters—is occupied by Mr. Torii Gekkyū, thirty-nine; his wife, thirty-four; and their sons, eight and ten. The visitor enters from the stairwell into the concrete-floored outer half of the entryway, shucks his footgear, and steps up to the raised wooden floor of the inner half. There are no decorations in the entryway, but it is cleaner and more orderly than such places usually are. An unpainted rack to the left holds assorted footgear, umbrellas, a softball and bat, and four badminton racquets. Baseball caps and school jackets hang above it. To the right a door opens into the toilet, another door into a broom closet.

Further in are the mat-floored rooms, their walls so heavily lined with furniture and equipment that one has a feeling of Pullman-style planned stowage. There are no armchairs, although they are found in some Hikari ga Oka apartments. In fact, some of the more affluent neighbors even spread rugs across the mats. But there is a serviceable low table in the center of the four-mat room, directly under the light fixture. In the six-mat room there are two tall clothes cabinets, their tops piled to the ceiling with layers of boxes. There is a chest of drawers, on it an electric fan and a souvenir model of Tokyo Tower. In one corner stands a treadle sewing machine. (One wall is taken up by closets for storing the bedding during the day.)

The four-mat room also holds two chests of drawers. Their tops afford the only display space, since these apartments lack the alcove so common to Japanese houses. One chest holds a fishbowl with two goldfish, and a homemade cloth doll with pink dress and corn-yellow hair. On the other chest are a late-model radio and a glass case containing two Japanese dolls. One is of a samurai in battle array, the other of Ninomiya Kinjirō. Half the kitchen is given over to cupboards, sink, and gas plate. The other half is carpeted with thin straw matting and has two straight chairs and study tables, each with its own lamp, a few books, and a model airplane.

Torii and his family came to Hikari ga Oka from what they describe as damp, dismal, rented rooms in a house in the older part of the city. There they had lived some six years, ever since he obtained a position in the Matsumoto Regional Office (branch office for the prefectural administration). He is the eldest son of an Anchiku farm household, and by Japanese ideals he should have succeeded his father on the farm. However, Torii had graduated from a university in Tokyo, and he had other ambitions. He did try his hand at farming for three years, then relinquished the succession to a younger brother and sought a salaried post. He was disappointed that he could do no better than the regional bureaucracy. He felt that with his Tokyo degree, even though it is not from one of the "ivy league" schools, he was qualified for one of the national bureaus. "The regional official is the worst off," he says. "They promise 8,000 yen starting salary for college graduates, but it doesn't work out to near that. On the one hand you read about salarymen in the securities companies getting a 300,000 yen annual bonus. And on the other hand you are forbidden to demonstrate for higher pay."

Government offices are closed on Saturday afternoons and Sundays. Public schools follow the same schedule, so the Torii family can all be at home together at least a day and a half a week. Evenings are less dependable, since Mr. Torii has late assignments two or three times a week. Occasionally, too, his office gang goes out for a drink after work, although their major sessions are on Saturday nights. They call themselves the "Saturday Meeting," and eight of them gather, by turns, at each others' homes. Each man contributes 300 yen per meeting; this the host uses to buy sake and food. "The meetings serve several purposes," Torii explains. "We all have an opportunity to unburden our gripes; we have a good time; we cheer each other up; and we're not tempted into gambling or into going 'stairstep drinking' from one bar to another."

Father and sons also are home on nine annual official holidays. Six of these days are passed much the same as Sundays. Only three of these days does the family celebrate—on New Year's Day, Constitution Day, and Children's Day. However, they also celebrate several unofficial annual occasions, among them the bean-throwing festival, Anchiku Girls' Day, the flowering of the local cherry trees, the midsummer festival, the Hikari ga Oka annual outing, the festival of the Matsumoto tutelary shrine, the boys' birthdays, and Christmas. On some of these occasions Torii is able to return from work early.

The Toriis are relatively celebratious—"the boys thrive on it so"—although in common with many Japanese they recognize the gap between what they prefer to celebrate and what the government encourages. Christmas, for example, though unofficial is favored. This is the secular Christmas, done in an American manner with presents, trees, Santa Claus, and jingle bells. It has become widespread in Japan in the modern century. The Torii sons play host to their parents on Christmas Eve, saving from their allowances to buy a tree, a Christmas cake, and gifts. The family gathers to hear Christmas music, eat cake, and open presents.

Currently there is no official national holiday on March 3, a day that popular tradition long had regarded as Girls' Day. This was one of the Tokugawa "Five Breaks." The adoption of the Gregorian calendar in the 1870's shattered the harmonies of the older ceremonial calendar, and the dissonances reverberate down to today. In most regions Girls' Day is celebrated on Gregorian March 3; in a very few regions it is celebrated on the third of the lunisolar third month; and in a number of regions, such as Anchiku, it is celebrated on Gregorian April 3. Thus, Anchiku has both a national and a local Girls' Day, and the Toriis like many of their neighbors celebrate both. However, they do so in their own way. April 3 they honor as the birthday of Mr. Torii's mother, inviting her to visit for the day. March 3 they honor as a family-devised "Mother's Break" (okāsan no sekku), and at the same time as their wedding anniversary. "It's the one day of the year," says Mr. Torii, "when you absolutely mustn't fight with your wife."

Sundays and holidays the whole family sleeps late—

ten o'clock or so—and Mrs. Torii foregoes routine morning dusting. The day passes without plan, reading, chatting with neighbors, puttering in the garden plot between the apartment blocks. Sometimes the family walks to one of the nearby parks, sometimes they go downtown shopping. "But we aren't like some of the families here who think they are deprived if they don't get out every Sunday."

Once a year Mr. Torii is off for a three-day vacation tour with an office group, to a national shrine or hot springs resort. The sons also have two annual school study tours of one or two-day duration. Mrs. Torii travels the least of all, although she does spend about three weeks every July at her parental home—taking the sons with her.

She is an Anchiku girl, daughter of a well-to-do farmer. Her life, like that of most salaryman wives, is taken up with household tasks and with supervising her children's schooling. She manages the family budget (Finance Minister, Mr. Torii calls her), and takes over the pay envelope after Mr. Torii has deducted a sum for his monthly expenses. She hands down allowances to the sons (one hundred yen for the elder, fifty for the younger), pays the regular monthly bills (newspaper, gas, electricity), makes savings and insurance deposits, and allocates the remainder to her various household accounts. "I don't try to count to the last yen. I know about how much to spend as the month goes along, and usually I manage to 'over' it a bit," she says, using an English word in vogue.

About half of the Hikari ga Oka families have electric refrigerators. The Toriis do not, so Mrs. Torii shops almost every day for fresh fruit and vegetables, and two or three times a week for fish. But, during the midday hours, when the morning chores are done, there is time for visiting with other wives. "These apartments get pretty boring at times."

Once a month she joins five other wives in a cloth-doll-making group. They too meet at each other's apartments by turns (the format is a common one for many kinds of Japanese small groups). Each wife contributes 100 yen per turn, and the accumulated fund is used once a year for an all-day outing for the six families. "The men get suitably drunk, the children play games, and the wives enjoy the spectacle."

Evenings, she supervises the boys' homework, or sews, or sometimes reads—the Matsumoto evening paper, the Asahi weekly, or *Kurashi no Techō*, a slick-paper house-and-garden magazine that she buys at reduced prices a month late. She thinks of joining the Mothers' Library, sponsored by the Peoples' Hall, but fears she could not read rapidly enough to complete books within the two-week lending period.

"We used to talk of having three children," she remarks, setting out a dish of peaches for the visitor. "But we probably will stop at two. We want both boys to go on to college. We're saving all we can for it, but, even so, how can we possibly manage to send two of them at once? The other day the younger one told me not to worry. He said he's going to get a scholarship for study in America."

The Toriis cannot afford private tutors, as can some of their neighbors. But both parents take an active interest in the boys' homework, and they send the boys to special classes. Every Sunday both boys attend for two hours a calligraphy class of seven, taught by a Regional Office co-worker who is an expert. And the oldest son joins an abacus class of twenty, also taught by a Regional

Office employee, every Monday, Wednesday, and Friday evening.

"Television?" asks the visitor. "Not yet," says Mrs. Torii. "The boys are allowed to watch two evenings a week, at the neighbor's across the hall. We've promised them we will buy a set in a year or so if they continue to do well in school."

The Farmer

Sir George Sansom's dictum has become the standard interpretation of Tokugawa farm policy. Sir George said that Tokugawa administrators "thought highly of agriculture, but not of agriculturalists." Actually, the same attitude characterized Japanese administration well into modern times. In the postwar years, however, an attitudinal watershed has been crossed, and the present-day farmer is truly one of the new men of modern Japan. The general populace still tends to see him as a rustic and an earthy reservoir of tradition—the dream of a village arcadia complete with electric lights and running water remains strong even in a vanguard novelist such as Mishima Yukio (in *The Sound of Waves*). And Western observers seem unable to call him anything but a peasant. But if he has not achieved enough economic rationality to satisfy the extension agents, he is not like the typical peasant who, in the words of Robert Redfield, "would rather keep the city at a distance."

The changeover should not be seen as sudden and revolutionary, although our nearness to it lends it drama. Nor should it all be credited to the Occupation-sponsored land reforms, although these were a critical factor. It should be seen as a long-term shift in the relative strengths of many forces that tended on the one hand to hold down, on the other hand to promote, the agrarian style of living.

On the one hand, the Tokugawa leaders viewed the peasant as little better than a revenue animal. He ranked somewhat above the craftsman or merchant, in theory, since he was the only one of the three who "produced." He was to be encouraged in this, but not coddled lest he grow restive. The aim was not to make him healthy, wealthy, and wise, but to keep him healthy, humble, and just slightly hungry. Agricultural taxes continued to supply more than half of government revenues down to 1900, and, for the most part, it was the Japanese farmer who bought Japan a modern industrial economy. Across the nation as a whole, agricultural acreage and the farming population remained at their 1868 levels until the Pacific War. Half the labor force was classed as agricultural, and at least a fair fragment of this class appears to have consisted of "disguised unemployment." Modern administrations have exploited the farm household as a social-security organ with apparently no more hesitation than Tokugawa lords showed in ordering village priests to provide elementary schooling and maintain population records. At one period in the 1920's "unemployment relief" consisted of offering one-way fares to those urbanites who had a family they could return to in the country. The agricultural standard of living was rising in the years before the war, but it was not rising so rapidly as that in industry or commerce. A revealing indicator is the curve of demand for rice. In the modern era, in periods of prosperity the income elasticity of demand for rice has tended to fall in urban areas, but to rise in rural areas. Even in recession periods urbanites have been able to buy sufficient rice, whereas farmers have felt obliged to subsist on coarser grain. One hears anecdotes, possibly untrue but indicative, of farm households which never had eaten rice regularly until it was distributed to them as part of wartime rationing.

On the other hand, forces tending to advance and to commercialize Japanese agriculture have been operative since the beginning of the Tokugawa period. It is doubtful whether the Japanese agriculturalist, except in isolated areas, deserves to be called a peasant after the beginning of the eighteenth century. From then down to today the standard productive unit has been the small holding, operated by a single family. Large holdings have existed, but they regularly have been parceled out to single-family renters rather than worked collectively. Rents often have been felt to be burdensome, and may have discouraged tenants from increasing their productivity lest the increase be taken from them as higher rent. But major complaints on this score have been removed by the recent land reforms. Technological improvements were by no means lacking even before the war (or in Tokugawa times for that matter). But in Japan, as in the United States in the past twenty years, agriculture has undergone what at close range looks to be a technological revolution. Better seed, chemical fertilizers and pesticides, power cultivators and threshers, professional advisory services—all add up to mean that an ordinary rice farmer today produces about double what he could produce before the war. His land is his own. He has opportunities for spare-time employment in stores and factories. There is heavy government investment in crop protection, waterworks, land reclamation. There are producers' coöperatives in nearly every village to market his crops, extend credit, and sell him tools and supplies at bulk rates. And there is reasonable hope of matching urban standards of living.

The change should not be exaggerated; it is more potential than present. Keeping the children down on the farm is no easy task, especially when you would just as soon they became salaried. But the outlook seems more optimistic than at any time in living memory.

Wifery

In contrast to the salaryman, the farmer shares with the merchant an entrepreneurial "bourgeois" spirit. He is, indeed, bound in some degree by the community social framework. At the very least he must not so offend his neighbors that they refuse him access to irrigation waters or to village-owned woodlots (which remain, even though illegal). But he need not be unduly friendly—ordinarily, of course, he prefers to be—as the salaryman and merchant must. And he may go for weeks with little more than casual contact with the neighbors.

The point is not that independence is good in itself. Rather it is that the farmer, like the merchant, has room to exploit his own and his household's labor power. They are more free to "moonlight" if they wish, to take outside jobs, to work longer hours with the assurance of at least a small increment of income. Where the salaryman is most sensitive to his social relationships with his work mates, the farmer and the merchant are most sensitive to the factors of household production. Agricultural productivity is rather dependable these days —over a long run probably no more capricious than the salaryman's employers, who may or may not promote him. So that the typical farmer looks especially to side employments for opportunities to increase his family's income.

The farmer's life thus is far less easy to segregate into

a work sphere and a family sphere. His wife works alongside him in the fields at most tasks, although the children are likely to join them only on weekends or during school vacations. But the farmer, or his wife, or perhaps a grown but unmarried child, is likely to be employed full-time elsewhere. (Today only one-third of Japanese farm families live entirely off crop income. Of the remainder, half derive the bulk of their income from nonfarming pursuits.) It is usual for the males to take the outside jobs, although women do on occasion. And usual for wives and daughters to take over the day-to-day farming tasks, the men assisting at peak periods. As Professor Tobata Seiichi has remarked, this can no longer be called husbandry; it has to be called "wifery."

A farm household's patterns of work and play are shaped by the village social framework, but again much less clearly than are the salaryman's. So great are the variations from family to family in combining agricultural and other jobs that demands for village unity as to working days and holidays are not easily enforced. Farming brings with it seasonal rushes and slack periods not so acutely felt by the merchant or the salaryman. But skillful management can level off all except the worst peaks and valleys in the annual curve of labor demand. The farmer does not routinely take off from work every Sunday, but he is probably more free than the salaryman, certainly more than the merchant, to set his work aside for a few days almost any time during the year.

Finally, like the merchant the farmer does have a position and an enterprise to transmit to his children. However, there is an uncertainty in this. Although agricultural productivity is rather predictable, agricultural markets are less so. In the past few years there has been anxiety over a possible rice glut and over changes in national tastes. There also have been many experiments with large-scale corporate dairying, poultry raising, and fruit growing. So there is reason to doubt whether the children should be encouraged to continue farming, on the one hand. And, on the other, there are hopes that they may win university degrees and enter the salaried ranks. More than one Anchiku farmer told me that he has been thinking of selling part of his paddy in order to send a son to college.

Hannō Kimben

About a mile from the Ariake business center, along a narrow graveled road that is companion to a twisting creek, you come upon yet another cluster of buildings. As you draw near, the cluster resolves into four weathered farmhouses with their satellite outbuildings, all huddled together three hundred yards from their nearest neighbors. For Anchiku it is a prosy sight. In the house nearest the road live Mr. Hannō Kimben and his family. Mr. Hannō's house is large and unwieldy, and so in a manner of speaking is his family. And that is the nub of his current situation.

Seven persons make up the household, only two of them able-bodied—Mr. Hannō and his wife, both forty-one. Their labors must support as well his parents—seventy-nine and seventy-three; and three school children, daughters—fourteen and twelve, and son—eight. Under its high thatched roof the house has five mat-floored rooms with a total of forty-two mats, plus a wood-floored kitchen about twelve by fifteen feet, a small bathroom, and a dirt-floored entry. Behind it is a combination granary and tool shed, in front a toilet and a chicken coop. Built in the second decade of this century, the house is nearing the end of its useful life. Like most Anchiku farmhouses of its vintage it was planned for silkworms as well as for people. Except in the sitting room, there are no ceilings: one looks up directly to the underside of the thatch. Until a few years ago when sericulture ceased to be a profitable side-line, in summer the house would be completely opened on the inside and silkworm trays hung in tiers from floor almost to roof. "Sometimes they even filled the sitting room," says Mr. Hannō. "Mother still raises a few silkworms, but now just as a kind of hobby."

The boards on the veranda have ends smoothly rounded from long use. On them are spread the parts of an automatic bird scare, opened and dismantled for maintenance. The visitor picks his path around them and is guided to the sitting room. Here even at midday the interior is cool and shaded by the roof overhang. The woodwork is richly blacked from years of open fires in the kitchen firepit. The shoji, patched many different times, are a study in chiaroscuro. The mats are a deep brown, sagging and worn. There is a plain table in the center of the room, and a chest against the one brown-plaster wall. The glass door of the chest is cracked, and the crack has been carefully mended with cut-paper stars. Through the glass one can read the title of a one-volume encyclopedia of Japanese history. Atop the chest is a shallow bowl with an arrangement of plum blossoms. On the wall behind are a clock and a calendar advertising an Ariake rice merchant. Above, hung from a corner of the ceiling, is a god-shelf laden with printed paper talismans from several shrines.

"We have more space than we know what to do

with," says Mr. Hannō. "We've talked of dividing one of the big rooms into study rooms for these two now that they are in middle school," he nods toward his daughters, who giggle impishly. "But we may as well wait now and rebuild from the ground up."

He has been head of the household for ten years. Although he is the eldest son, he had intended to relinquish the succession to his younger brother. He had picked up some forestry training before the war; during and after the war he was foreman in a charcoal factory in Yamanashi. At the time of his marriage fifteen years ago he looked forward to a factory career. But the company went bankrupt two years later, and Mr. Hannō brought his family to his father's house while he sought another position. His father at the time was eager to retire, and urged him to assume headship, at least for a few years.

Mr. Hannō has no fondness for working in the fields. He prefers the months from December to April when he is off daily to the foothills, subcontracting as a maker of soft charcoal. Not that he is indifferent to his paddies, for they provide the better half of his income. But he plans his crop season as reasonably as possible; he paces his work in the fields by clock. He relies heavily upon suggestions from the agricultural extension agent, who inspects his paddies periodically and who offers detailed directions regarding fertilizers and insecticides and optimum times for transplanting and harvesting.

He sees no need for the sunup to sundown routine still favored by some farmers. "Except for a couple of weedings and a dusting, you might just as well leave the crop alone most of the summer." He works from eight to twelve in the morning with a half-hour break at ten. After lunch he works until 5:30 with another half-hour break at 3:30. Occasionally he may work later to complete the day's task. In the heat of summer he naps from after lunch until about 2. And while the paddies are under water (June into August) he must check the water levels daily at 7:00 A.M. and 6:00 P.M.

The work has its seasonal changes, which lend it variety. But apart from the maelstrom period at spring transplanting—Ariake farmers contract for transplanting hands six months to a year in advance—Mr. Hannō is able to avoid major changes in his routine. He feels he can never slack off for long, with so many to support. And on the other hand he feels he must never overwork himself to the brink of illness. Many farmers use rainy days as rest days, but on rainy days Mr. Hannō turns to the third of his enterprises: he drafts house plans for local carpenters, who pay a commission. Only on seven or eight annual holidays will he permit himself a full nonworking day. (However there are some fourteen other occasions during the year which the family celebrates after hours.) Twice a year he joins a one-day outing, in spring with the carpenters' association, in autumn with neighbors.

On holidays he shares a bottle of sake with his father. But he feels he cannot afford a regular evening cup, as do many of his neighbors. Evenings he usually is at home. He rarely attends village meetings, other than the hamlet's annual plenary session. Nor is he active in the producers' coöperative. "I'm a member in name only. I'd rather have K—— handle my rice and supply my fertilizer. He charges a shade more, but he also furnishes pickup and delivery service, which the coöperative does not. I don't need any crop loans, although sometimes I borrow a little from my brother in charcoal season."

55

Some evenings he returns to his drafting; once or twice a month goes to watch a neighbor's television. Mostly he devotes himself to his one consuming interest, historical collecting. Ever since he can remember, he has been assembling old items, anything that seems curious or interesting. Apart from an heirloom sword none of the items has much cash value. But with donations from friends and relatives he gradually has accumulated a considerable number of coins, stamps, jewelry, even antique appliances such as vegetable-oil lamps. He studies and assembles his items in ways that aptly illustrate the utility of petty history. His thirty-year collection of cigarette packages, for example. By noting changes in the quality of paper and print—he tells the visitor—and by noting the reasons for commemorative issues, one can easily follow the drift of recent national history: the rise of militarism, early victories, late wartime scarcity, the Occupation, and finally recovery and relative abundance.

His wife, daughter of a tailor in Yamanashi, had worked as clerk in a clothing store until their marriage was arranged. After ten years on the farm she still considers herself a city girl. She occasionally helps Mr. Hannō in the paddies, but says that she is too clumsy to be useful. "The only farm task I can manage decently is feeding the chickens," she says. But most of her daytime hours are taken up with meals, laundering, mending, and with looking after the old folks. Like a good young wife, she is first to rise in the morning and last to go to bed at night.

She still does not feel at ease with most village women. For a while she tried participating in Women's Club affairs but soon wearied of them. "Never anything but politely trivial chatter," she explains. She feels isolated, but has few opportunities to go out: in summer, to visit her parents; half a dozen times a year, to shop for a day in Matsumoto; one evening a month, to the free movie in the People's Hall; and one evening a month to a neighborhood young wives' club. Since all members are young wives, the group is partly a share-the-misery association. But like so many other Japanese organizations of its kind, it combines utility and enjoyment. Each woman contributes 500 yen per meeting. The sum is enough to buy one service-grade quilt. With twelve members, each receives one quilt per year.

The daughters sometimes lend a hand with household tasks. But most of their out-of-school hours are given over to study and play. They do not have regular study desks, but Mr. Hannō has rigged crates and boards into a makeshift study corner in one of the little-used rooms. Most evenings the girls turn to homework, often with Mrs. Hannō supervising. But Tuesdays and Sundays they are allowed to watch television at a neighbor's. They are not expected to perform any heavy farm tasks. "Anybody who worked his kids hard these days would be gossiped about as feudalistic," says their mother.

Mr. Hannō does not expect his children to continue at farming. He wants them all to find positions with good companies. If their teachers pronounce them capable, he will send them on to high school (which is not compulsory). Otherwise he will rely heavily upon the middle school teachers and their contacts to find suitable positions for his children. His hope is that, after the children are employed, he and his wife can return to the city, taking his parents along. He believes that, because of his training and years of experience, he will qualify for a good position despite his age. "Farming," he sums up, "is no longer a decent way to live.

But I don't think my younger brother cares to take over the farm either. . . ."

The Merchant

The city merchant is the middleman of modern Japan in more than the usual commercial sense of the word. His style of living is between those of the salaryman and the farmer, has influenced both of them, and has changed the least of all three. Its contents have changed vastly, of course. The industrial revolution has brought mass communications facilities to his home and the fruits of mass production to his display shelves. But anyone who has read the seventeenth century bourgeois novels of Saikaku need make no mental recalibrations to understand the twentieth-century merchant in Matsumoto.

The Tokugawa merchant tradition gave birth to two of the notable characteristics of Japanese modernism, its commercial knowhow and its sense of joy in living. The samurai provided administrative skills and an assurance of moral purpose. The peasants supplied the material wherewithal. The merchants added a third essential in the form of an ear attuned to the changing melodies of the marketplace, and a hand accustomed to giving and taking money. (The samurai was morally above, the peasant materially below, an easy familiarity with money and its uses.)

At the same time the merchants, with the aid of their fellow townsmen, brought forth a moral model that remains the chief competitor to the samurai-spartan ideal. To put it oversimply, if the samurai paragon must be ever ready to die, the proper townsman must be ever ready to live. There is little doubt that life in the

58

Tokugawa cities was loud and lusty. It was loudest in the "floating world" of the "nightless cities," the pleasure quarters, but its reverberations spread into every street and alley, and were echoed even from the countryside. Most of what is recognizably "Japanese" in present-day Japanese mass culture derives from the mass culture of the Tokugawa cities—kabuki, sumō, geisha houses, sexy novels, gaudy paintings, the samisen (an Okinawan import), puppet theater, or the Osaka songs known as *Naniwa-bushi*. Even today the urbane man follows Tokugawa tastes. As Robert J. Smith says:

"The man of *tsū* [expertise] in Tokyo, Osaka, and Kyoto takes his cue about where to purchase certain things from the prejudices of the older chōnin tradition to a surprising extent. He will invariably know the famous *noren* (shop curtains) of the specialty houses which only in the past few years have condescended to establish branch shops in the new downtown districts of commerce and entertainment. He knows that the best bean candy in Tokyo is to be had at Toraya and Shioze. For dried seaweed he will recommend Morihan in Tokyo's Omori district or Yamamotoya in Nihonbashi. In Osaka, he must buy his seaweed at Oguraya, and he will try to get his Japanese cakes at Surugaya or Tsuruya. There are kimono-makers and kimono accessories shops like Daihiko, Tatsumura, and Erihan and certain restaurants like Edogin in Tsukiji, Yabusoba in Kanda and Eisaka known to the man of tsū. In Tokyo there are a number of spots which are very old, very inexpensive and which have a single specialty: a cake called *sakura-mochi* is nowhere better than at a small shop near the Chōmeiji on the Sumida River and the mud-fish at the Asakusa restaurant called Komagata is unexcelled. . . ."

Japanese moralists for three centuries have cried shame upon such urbanity. So have administrators, for the floating world and its popular culture have continually threatened to drown salaryman, merchant, and farmer alike. Indeed one cannot help but suspect that the very vigor of the repeated waves of moral rearmament over these centuries—Shingaku among the Tokugawa merchants and Ninomiya's Hōtoku among the peasants, or perhaps Tenrikyō across the nation today—is more than anything a response to the seductive lure of city lights.

The Market Melody

The merchant style of living is overwhelmingly similar to that of the now-commercialized farmer. As we have seen, the two resemble each other on various points: in comparison with the salaryman, both farmer and merchant are more independent of social ties but less financially secure; both incorporate the labor of other family members in their work; both find it more difficult to segregate their work and play; both have a heritable enterprise and social position.

However we can distinguish the merchant's style from the farmer's on several counts (apart from his more immediate participation in urban culture). Perhaps most critical is that where the farmer is attuned to the rhythms of seasonal production the merchant is attuned to the more rapid fluctuations of the market. He must heed seasonal variations, but he is more directly mindful of the diurnal swings and sways of supply and demand. Furthermore, a sense of competition is ever present. The farmer struggles to better last year's harvest, the salaryman to outdistance his peers. The merchant is in daily combat both against his rivals and against last week's, or month's, or year's, sales volume. It is a rare man who would be bold enough to close his shop on a day when his competitors are open. And advocates of Sunday-closing agreements encounter many of the same problems that face American advocates of Sunday blue laws.

Then too the merchant must exploit his personality somewhat more, or at any rate in different ways, than the farmer. Ward organizations make relatively few demands upon him these days, and presumably it would not matter if he were at odds with his neighbors. But the merchant must maintain amicable ties, on the one hand, with his regular customers and, on the other, with the regular jobbers and wholesalers upon whom he depends not only for goods but as well for short-term credit. On balance this may or may not allow less psychic freedom than the farmer has—for village gossip is an endemic complaint—but it surely is less constricting than the company's grip upon the salaryman.

Eitai Machi

Stores and workshops exist today in nearly all parts of Matsumoto, but in Tokugawa times the merchants and craftsmen occupied a zone outside the castle walls. They were segregated more or less by occupation into neighborhoods that had, like the Tokugawa village, a fair degree of self-government. The imprint of the plan still is readily visible to him who walks the streets with a knowing eye.

Eitai Machi is a side street three blocks long, walled on either hand by tight-fitted rows of narrow store dwellings. The buildings rarely are more than twenty feet wide, but they stand upon lots that are up to 150 feet deep. The store or office is in front; the family lives in back or upstairs. Behind the building there sometimes is a godown or workshop, sometimes a garden. Most of the buildings date from before the Pacific War, and a few have the low roofs and setback second floors that went out of vogue in Anchiku around the turn of the century.

On old maps Eitai Machi is listed as a craftsmen's quarter. It retains some of this aura, and is drab, its signs unimposing and bereft of neon in contrast to signs on the main retail streets three blocks away. The majority of its 173 households engage in some form of craftwork or family production, although none of them claims continuous residence since the Tokugawa period. (More than half of them have moved in since the end of the war.) But there is great diversity in the trades: several jobbers and wholesalers, tinsmiths, cabinetmakers, a saw-filer, a typewriter repairman, and a shop where milk is processed semiautomatically into a sweet, fruit-flavored drink called "yogurt." (In Japanese *yakuruto*. The operator has a franchise from a national organization which in its advertising chooses to spell the name Yakult.) In addition there are several small food shops; these cater mostly to a neighborhood clientele.

Akinai Majime

At night or on holidays, when wooden shutters cover all the shops, one can scarcely tell where one building leaves off and the next begins. But most days from 6:30 A.M. until 10:30 P.M. one can readily pick out the white-washed interior three doors from the main thoroughfare. It is the grocery operated by Mr. Akinai Majime, forty-four, and his wife, thirty-eight. (They have sons, eleven and five, and a daughter, nine).

The store is small, and crowded with goods: tables piled with fresh fruit and vegetables, shelves of canned goods, candy and crackers in glass jars, a foot-square ice-cream freezer at the street's edge. One has to slip sideways to reach the back. Here on the right are kitchen and toilet, with a steep narrow ladder leading to the second story and its two eight-mat rooms. On the left downstairs are a six-mat sitting room, and a six-mat room where the cashbox and records are kept, where Mr. Akinai and his wife rest when no customers are in the shop, and where the family takes its meals.

The latter room is cluttered with newspapers, boxes of unshelved goods, and bundles of bills. It bears the marks of heavy wear. But in the sitting room, further from the store, the mats are new and crisp. In one corner is a television set, covered with a heavy cloth, in another corner a table holding a glass fishtank with seven gold-fish. There is a rather conventional mountains-and-water painting in the alcove, with a potted plant in front of it. The two chests against the wall are matched and modern, with recessed drawer pulls and a limed-oak finish. Over them hangs a framed color photograph of the Crown Prince and Princess Michiko in their formal wedding robes.

"There's room enough in this house," says Mrs. Akinai, pouring glasses of orange soda for the visitor and for her husband, who arises from his afternoon nap in the front room. She pours a shotglass full for the youngest son, then warns him that if he doesn't quit slurping it he'll get a bellyache. "But the space is badly organized. Some-day we may rebuild with an eye to convenience."

Mr. Akinai has been in business here for thirteen years.

As younger son of an Anchiku landlord and politician he had been sent first to agricultural high school and later, at his own urging, to a Tokyo commercial high school. Soon after graduation he enlisted in the army, and spent most of his three years in Manchuria and North China. Upon discharge he became a clerk in a Matsumoto tool works, but he was recalled during the Pacific War. After the war he worked as clerk in a large paper wholesale firm. But in two years he found himself weary of petty office routines and decided to enter business himself.

"It's nice to be a company man, wear a suit, and have social security. But I had my fill of being pushed around in the army. Business is more of a challenge; you have to have the heart to calmly watch a box of fruit stand unsold for several days until it rots."

With other Matsumoto grocers, he closes his shop on the "sixes" of the month, the 6th, 16th, and 26th days. (The pattern can be traced to the Tokugawa period.) Almost every other day of the year—New Year's Day is the notable exception—he is away by 7:30 each morning to place his orders at the city wholesale produce market and with his other suppliers. He is back by 11:00 A.M., when the goods arrive, and he spends an hour or so preparing them for display. He lunches, naps, and lounges until after 4:00 P.M. when the evening rush brings in the heaviest trade of the day.

Business drops off after seven. He has a few cups of sake before dinner, and sometimes is joined by his wife. After dinner he goes to the public bath, watches TV, deals with the straggle of late customers, and reads his newspapers. He subscribes regularly to four: a Tokyo daily and a Matsumoto daily, a national business daily and a sports sheet.

The routine is compelling but not without its conveniences. He cannot afford to neglect his daily buying and selling. But, apart from the hectic days just before festivals and holidays, he almost always can find free moments and even free afternoons. He estimates that he reads his newspapers for a total of two hours a day, although rarely for more than half an hour at any one time. And he can fairly easily arrange a few hours to go see a high school baseball game or visit his parents in the country. He does not often travel outside of Anchiku, although he wishes he could. But he does join every year in a three-day sight-seeing tour sponsored by the members of the wholesale produce market, who all close shop for the occasion. And two or three times a year the whole family goes for a day's outing in Anchiku.

The enterprise is simple enough to require only an ordinary daily recording of income and outgo. It is stable enough to provide the Akinai family with a comfortable, if by no means sumptuous, standard of living. "We usually figure twelve or thirteen thousand yen a month for living expenses. But of course we can eat at wholesale, and every so often we feel obliged to eat up something that otherwise would just spoil. Anyway, we aren't in debt. There was enough in savings to pay for repairing typhoon damage to the roof last year without needing to take out a loan. I get along with credit from the brokers and the wholesalers. I have to pay the wholesalers the first and fifteenth of the month, and the brokers every other day. I know I could be making a good deal more if I rushed around, but why wear yourself out?"

Mr. Akinai conducts most of the sales himself. He says that an average day yields about one hundred transactions. One third of these are with steady customers, mainly from Eitai Machi. Another third are with occasional customers, and the remainder with irregulars and passers-by. About a dozen families have continued to buy from him regularly ever since he opened the shop.

The son began to sing the theme song for "Colt 45" but was shushed by his mother.

Like many merchant wives, Mrs. Akinai (under her husband's surveillance) is bookkeeper. She posts the daily figures, works out monthly balances, deposits savings, pays insurance installments, and hands out allowances to the older children. "We follow the standards set by the school and the PTA, but this doesn't really fit our case. Our children can walk into the shop anytime and help themselves to things other children have to pay for." She tends the shop when her husband is away, and she helps him when customers congregate, but the burden of labor is upon him. "I'm not a good business woman," she says. "I find it hard to take when some of these small-hearted wives begin to complain that somebody six blocks away is selling melons for two yen cheaper. Or people who don't take the time to read price tags carefully, then gripe because maybe you are pricing by weight instead of by piece. However, they've been getting better in recent years. Ten years ago even some of the regular customers would go elsewhere because of a two yen difference."

Like most merchant wives, she arises in the morning to remove the shutters and start breakfast before the rest of the family awakes. The daughter helps her clean the living rooms; the older son helps his father sweep out the shop. Trade is slow on the usual morning—a dozen sales or so—so that after the older children have left for school and her husband for the market, Mrs. Akinai takes up her daily washing and household chores. Afternoons she usually watches the shop while her husband naps, but she can easily arrange an hour or two to visit friends or to go shopping. And once or twice a month, when the mood strikes her, she may go to a movie. (Her youngest son, of course, accompanies her on all these outings.)

Evenings after bathing, bedding down the youngest son, washing the dishes, she does her daily bookkeeping. After that she watches TV (is fond of quiz shows such as "My Secret" or comedies such as "I Love Lucy"), checks the children's homework, or sews. Occasionally she goes out to a Labor Chorus concert, occasionally to a meeting of the Eitai Machi Women's Club.

The children do their homework in one of the upstairs rooms, when not watching television. Mr. and Mrs. Akinai expect the children to go to high school under any circumstances, but probably not to college, unless government aid becomes available. Mr. Akinai is not encouraging his son to learn the business, and says he would prefer it if the boy becomes a company man. "Anyway, I still think hard now and then about going overseas again. It's too bad that Manchuria is closed now; Brazil seems sort of far. But maybe I'm getting too old. By this time you begin to drop your dreams."

4. Work and the Framework

The scene was repeated many tens of times, and every time the first and last words of greeting were:

"Mr. Ōgiya, are you *enjoying* your American tour?"

"Well, Mr. Ōgiya, I hope you *enjoy* your plane trip from here."

At first, whenever I heard the word enjoy I was struck by a feeling of strangeness. In our daily lives the word enjoy has a special position. With its meaning of "finding pleasure in" or perhaps of "being merry about" this word—at least to those of my generation—has nuances that smack of the immoral. . . .

There are unemployed in America. In England and Italy there are crowds of the poor. What I mean to say is that in these countries the word enjoy has firmly put down roots into people's daily lives whether they have money or not. It is so to speak a basic principle of their attitude toward living—this is the point I'm trying to make. . . .

Since returning to Japan I've been tremendously bothered by this word. The thought often has occurred to me, haven't we possibly mistaken the purpose of daily living—or of existence?

ŌGIYA SHŌZŌ

68

The Japanese also do not find it easy to capture their modern selves in an image. In their own minds' eyes they appear in many figures and many masks—the selfless mother, the tireless student, the fearless samurai, to name but three. Some of these images are coated with sophistication and refinement, although most of them have the well-scrubbed glow of simplicity and renunciation. And in the earlier phases of the modern era one of the most popular (and popular*ized*) images was that of the "peasant sage" Ninomiya Kinjirō. Standard equipment in the prewar schoolyard included a statue of the young Ninomiya reading as he shuffled along with his back bent under a load of firewood. And standard dogma in the prewar catechisms included praises to his piety and energy. Here is a representative homily:

> Cutting brushwood,
>   making plain straw sandals;
> Lending a hand to parents,
>   helping elder brother;
> Brothers in harmony
>   tireless in filial piety:
> The model is Ninomiya Kinjirō!

During the war the statues were melted down, and after the war the textbooks were revised, but the image itself lives on. In the tart words of Tanabe Shin'ichi, "The postwar generation has been emancipated from this kind of agrarianistic moral textbook. But in fact, although the textbooks have disappeared, the psychological environment built upon a belief in themselves as the world's most diligent people—the *self-flattery*, that is, of enduring on heavy labor and low wages—has not even been shaken in the least." There is a difference, though. For in the process Ninomiya has been converted from a praiseworthy model to a pejorative one.

The Ninomiya image calls up American parallels with Poor Richard husbanding his time and money or with the black-robed Puritan preaching Christ and plowing corn. And indeed morals teachers both in Japan and in America accent versions of what Max Weber terms "inner-worldly asceticism." In both traditions producing is championed and playing is circumscribed. But this occurs for somewhat different reasons. It means, therefore, that, in examining the search for enjoyment in present-day Japan, we must take our cues from Ninomiya rather than from Poor Richard, lest we misconstrue the Japanese viewpoint. We begin with a sketch of the Japanese ideal. And we begin with the impression suggested by our chapter title: namely, that what is central in the Japanese view is not so much "work" in a Puritan sense; what is central is the social framework. In vernacular Japanese this could be condensed into a pun: the key word is not "work" (the Japanese use the Anglo word, pronouncing it *wāku*), the key word is the system of social control, the *waku*.

A Selective Orientation

First, a few remarks as to intent. I am going to outline some of the features of the dominant Japanese ideal as the ideal has developed in recent times. My approach is anthropological in the heritage of Ruth Benedict—I differ with her on some points that need not trouble us here—looking upon a culture as the sort of "orientation to experience" that is characteristic of a specific human community. To borrow the words of Clyde Kluckhohn, a culture in this sense refers to "those *selective* ways of feeling, thinking, and reacting that distinguish one group from another—ways that are socially transmitted and learned (with, of course, some changes through time) by each new generation."

Contrast is implicit in such an approach, and I contrast the Japanese ideal against a generalized American one. In such binary contrasts the amount of difference probably always tends to be overdone, the vast amount of similarity underdone. But the forewarned reader can arm in advance.

Furthermore, what is distinctively Japanese is the general orientation, the "configuration." Any or all of its individual features might be found in other cultures. It is the way the features are accented and orchestrated that becomes Japanese.

This is the dominant configuration. The human stuff is put up in many packages: the dominant ideal in any culture encompasses only a few of these, and the others are ignored or actively discouraged. The dominant cluster tends to be "enforced" both internally by the socialized individual and externally by what we might call for short (after Eliot in *The Cocktail Party*) the guardians. One result of this enforcement is the creation of a minimum amount of necessary standardization—often much less than one might expect—that dampens random swings of conduct. But enforcement has also another result. It is not a mechanical process but a human one. What is disvalued does not for that reason drop away. As the Freudians put it, the repressed material continues to return. The disvalued feelings, thoughts, and reactions continue in latent form and are likely to be favored openly by some individuals and groups. To the extent that this is so, personal ambivalence and social discord are inescapable features of the human condition. Perhaps enforcement and standardization are greater in some cultures than others, but the evidence is unconvincing. Nor is

71

there much ground for assuming—the view was popular in the West during the Pacific War—that the Japanese are more standardized than any other population. The Japanese dominant ideal has powerful rivals, and one of our tasks will be to examine these alternatives as well.

This is the dominant ideal. It is how the good Japanese ought to behave, the goals he should strive for even though he may not—perhaps in the usual instance cannot—attain. It is an abstraction from reality, but not divorced from it. It shades off into arcadia and utopia, but it is not merely arcadian or utopian: it is continually in use for judging self and others.

Finally, it is the recent ideal. Some of its elements can be traced to early Japanese history, but even these have undergone shifts in accent from time to time. Egalitarianism is a good example. In the Tokugawa era it was on the whole disvalued, although approved in limited contexts. But in earlier epochs it appears to have had higher general favor—as it does again today. Today one meets not a few Japanese who regard the Tokugawa and early modern era preference for hierarchy as something of an aberration. The primordial Japanese ideal, they argue, is to be discovered in the Heian epoch, in the age of the *Man'yōshū* when Emperor and serving girl could openly sit together writing poems. The new is but a rediscovery of the old.

The World and the Waku

The first thing we learn from the Ninomiya image is that in the dominant Japanese ideal the important world is this world. Throughout much of their history the Japanese have been rather indifferent to conceivable existences other than the present one, hazy about their details, and not given to seeking latter-day rewards in them. Witness Japanese reactions to alien teachings. Confucian doctrines, with their focus upon human right-conduct, were warmly received and eagerly propagated. Taoism, with its more metaphysical and mystical bias, won few adherents. Buddhism in Japan came to center upon the teaching of compassion and of the search for enlightenment in the here and now. The original Indian vision of karma, of a perdurable soul advancing and retreating through many existences—"coming of age in the universe" as Huston Smith calls it—all but dropped away.

Another way to put this is that this world is the *real* world. The Japanese outlook favors the perceptible and the concrete, the fluid character of events more than the rigidity of abstraction. As Hajime Nakamura puts it in philosophical terms, the Japanese tend to "regard the phenomenal world itself as the Absolute and to reject the recognition of an Absolute existing over and above the phenomenal world. What is widely known among post-Meiji philosophers as the 'theory that the phenomenal is actually the real' has a deep root in Japanese tradition."

Next the Ninomiya image tells us—if we notice how the homily dwells upon parents and brothers—that what is especially real about this world is its social ties. Japanese reality is a political reality. It seems closer to the classical Greek idea of politics as the essence of human action than to the modern Western idea of equating the business of life with business. "The Japanese," says Nakamura, "look upon man as a being subordinated to a specific and limited human nexus; they conceive him in terms of human relations."

Not only is man in this human nexus, this waku, he is subordinated to it. The social framework takes precedence morally and in some senses even ontologically. Individuals are transient, communities permanent. Even the emperor is but the current manifestation of an unbroken line of emperors existing from time eternal. The head of a household is but the incumbent in an everlasting line of heads of household. It is perhaps a being-in-becoming orientation, in the categories sometimes used in the study of values. The individual is not a free agent apart from the nexus, in obvious contrast to the Rousseauvian individual who "enters" into the social contract. To overstate the case, Western ideals honor the rugged individual who sticks to his rights no matter what; Japanese ideals shame him as one of the worst of malefactors. He is guilty, as one modern Japanese phrase has it, of "nihilistic" selfishness.

Furthermore, this nexus tends to be limited and specific. There are, of course, generalized norms of decency, but there is no strong assertion that one must love neighbor as self and treat all men as equally children of God. The Japanese conscience seems rather less a "generalized other" than a constellation of known others. In the words of George DeVos, "certain types of psychological security found in a relationship to a personal God in the West are found only in relation to the actual family in Japan."

Within this limited nexus the ideal man's loyalty is absolute. No other ideals should have precedence. What in the West tend more to be held as "universal" ideals—truth, beauty, justice—in Japan tend more to be relative to the nexus. The good man should at all times stand ready to eschew the more universal when it conflicts with the more specific. The Japanese usually express this loyalty not in terms of devotion to the group as an abstraction but to the group's living, real head. And headship

74

tends to be a representative role more so than an executive one. For example the emperor is "sacred and inviolable"; if something is rotten in the state the ministers must be at fault. Collectivity heads in Japan have almost never been granted the degree of absolute power gripped by the stereotypic Asian despot. The head of a household has never had powers of capital punishment, as was true in Imperial China. Furthermore, Japanese devotion to the head is devotion to the head-as-status. One might also feel deep attraction to the head-as-person; but even if one did not, one should remain loyal.

Perhaps because the head is so vital as group symbol, the Japanese ideal tends to deny that loyalty is in any way conditional. All Japanese just "naturally" are loyal to the emperor, all samurai to their lord, all family members to their head. Look at this in contrast to the Chinese view of emperorship. The Chinese emperor was addressed as Son of Heaven, and his right to the throne depended upon his having won the mandate of Heaven. Should popular unrest occur, or even gross natural disaster, this might be a sign that Heaven was displeased and was withdrawing the mandate. The people then were empowered to remove the emperor and replace him with one more acceptable to Heaven. Japanese theorists continually scorned this view. The Japanese emperor, they argued, need not "receive" a mandate from Heaven, he already has it. He is not the son of Heaven, he "is" Heaven. Indeed, in the eyes of some Japanese writers the way that the Chinese theory leaves a door open to rebellion is a sign of moral inadequacy. There is an old popular anecdote which relates how *The Book of Mencius*, which advocates the right of popular rebellion, reached Japan only after many tribulations. Ships bearing the book from China, says the anecdote, were repeatedly blown from the coast of Japan by the *kamikaze,* the "divine wind" which has so often defended the islands.

Not only is loyalty absolute, it is active. It must be energetically lived out. Only the few may be chosen to live it out in high drama, like the suicide pilot; but the many are called to live it out in humble daily tasks, like Ninomiya Kinjirō. Loyalty is an obligation to be repaid. The debt is incurred because of the many benefits which membership in the group bestows upon the individual. This is not a matter for contractual calculation. No one can ever fully repay the debt. It is, as one Japanese phrase puts it, higher than the mountains and deeper than the sea.

Here I find it helpful to adopt an organizational paradigm which John Pelzel has set forth in his lectures on Japanese society. Pelzel suggests that group action in Japan is based upon three premises:

One, the group is oriented towards achievement—towards attaining, not simply towards maintaining some status quo.

Two, it is oriented towards group achievement—towards group goals, not simply the goals of one or another of its members.

Three, tasks and rewards are allocated by status—all members must perform and all performances are essential, even though some are more "visible" than others.

This is an organic outlook upon society. Individuals are expected to hold personal feelings, thoughts, and reactions, but they are also expected to hold them in whenever they might endanger group achievement. Group harmony is important to the extent that it contributes to group achievement, but harmony per se is not an "ultimate" goal in the way it appears to have been, for example, in Imperial China. A happy family is desirable, but family members' performance is not conditional upon happiness. In Lord Avebury's terms, the Japanese ideal has stressed the Happiness of Duty much more than the Duty of Happiness.

It is the group's goals that matter most, and what matters about them is that they are the group's goals, regardless of their "content." They usually will be expressed as the wishes or decisions of the head, but it is taken for granted that the head will not announce merely selfish wishes but only those which have group consensus. For the head himself is as subordinate to group goals as any other member—usually phrased as his obligation to repay his ancestors—and, furthermore, he is expected to set an example for the rest.

Status alone does not justify. The very old and the very young are for the most part exempted from onerous demands, but all others must perform according to the "job description" of their status. One should be diligent about the tasks allotted to his status and satisfied by the rewards which accrue to it. Nor does status accrue without some demonstration of fitness. For example, ideally the eldest son succeeds his father as household head. (If no son is born, one is adopted.) But what this means in practice is that he has first crack at winning the post. Should he prove inferior he will be passed over, even though this may require adoption of a son as future head. (About one in five eldest sons is passed over.) Demands for proof of fitness begin to grow strong by the time a child is in school. And it is indeed a poor and overcrowded Japanese family that does not manage to provide a private desk and often a separate study room; at least a study-corner—often the only personal "private" spaces in the home—for each child student, even those in primary school. Japanese students have won a world reputation for diligence, and again the model is Nino-miya Kinjirō.

And the Repressed Self

The ideal thus is to unify the self with the others who are in the nexus. This I take it is what is implied in the Japanese slogan "extinguish the self and serve the group" (*metsuga hōkō*). And *this* is the sense in which the Japanese ideal lifts up duty and diligence as the cardinal virtues, while casting down selfishness and sloth as the cardinal vices.

This accent upon the unimportance of the self and its desires shows up in many ways. For example, Nakamura reports a folk etymology sometimes used by the Buddhist teachers. They explain that the common word *akirameru* ("to give something up; to resign oneself to") derives from the equally familiar phrase *akiraka ni miru*, which means "to see clearly, to understand explicitly." Again in some contexts in overt and formal social interaction, the Japanese tend to judge one another rather less as individuals than as representatives of groups. The community meeting is a good instance. In it there ordinarily is one vote per household, in contrast to the American ideal of the Town Meeting with one vote per adult male or even per adult individual. Ordinarily the head of a household attends the Japanese community meeting himself. But should any other member go in his stead, even a young daughter, she is assumed to speak and vote for her group as a whole.

There is some evidence that this ideal of self-repression reflects even from within Japanese personality structure. Some psychiatrically trained observers have suggested that—metaphorically—the boundaries of the Japanese self are more permeable than are those of the Western self, more open to "penetration" by other selves. As William Caudill has pointed out, there are no ready translation equivalents in English for this sort of interpersonal process. What words we can apply to it all seem loaded with overtones of aggressiveness—penetration, incorporation, devouring. The usual Japanese term for it has much softer connotations—*tokekomu*, literally "to melt into; to dissolve into." The word is widely used when appraising selves, and the ability to easily dissolve into a nexus is a prized one.

The Japanese do not pretend that so sublimating the self is any easy matter. For although the self be transient, yet it is real. With all of its feelings, thoughts, and reactions it is wholly of this world. Its flesh is not of the Tempter and, therefore, corrupt. And at this point the Ninomiya image diverges both from the Puritan and from the Indian Buddhist. Ruth Benedict has set forth this divergence succinctly: "An ethical code like Japan's, which requires such extreme repayment of obligations and such drastic renunciations, might consistently have branded personal desire as an evil to be rooted out from the human breast. This is the classical Buddhist doctrine and it is therefore doubly surprising that the Japanese code is so hospitable to the pleasures of the five senses. . . . The Japanese do not condemn self-gratification. They are not Puritans. They consider physical pleasures good and worthy of cultivation. They are sought and valued. Nevertheless, they have to be kept in their place. They must not intrude upon the serious affairs of life."

If man must live by the sweat of his brow it is not because he once Fell, it is because he is always Bound in the nexus. There is no Old Adam to be extirpated. The self is pure, although it tends to become corrupted so that its rust must periodically be polished away. A tragic sense of life, as Unamuno calls it, would not in Japanese eyes be one of cosmic suffering and emptiness. Rather it would be a sense of the joy of living crushed under the weight of the social framework—note Ōgiya Shōzō's reflections, in the chapter motto, on the word "enjoyment." Or as Nakamura phrases it, "Ours is different from the pessimism of the Occidental people. In the West pessimism means to become wearied of existence in this world. In the case of the Japanese, in contrast, it means to be wearied only of complicated social fetters and restrictions from which they wish to be delivered."

Evil, then, in the Japanese view is a sort of social friction. The man who can free himself of it can live out a smooth and frictionless life of perpetual emotion. The fundamental problem is to gear the self's desires into society's demands. When the two mesh, the self runs free, untroubled by selfish awareness. The Japanese dilemma of virtue is not so much one of choosing between good and evil as it is one of fusing together two things which *both* are good. On this point again Ruth Benedict summarizes the dilemma and its resolution in words worth repeating: The Japanese, she writes, "define the supreme task of life as fulfilling one's obligations. They fully accept the fact that repaying *on* [obligation] means sacrificing one's personal desires and pleasures. The idea that the pursuit of happiness is a serious goal of life is to them an amazing and immoral doctrine. Happiness is a relaxation in which one indulges when one can, but to dignify it as something by which the State and family should be judged is quite unthinkable. The fact that a man often suffers intensely in living up to his obligations . . . . is no more than they expect. It makes life hard but they are prepared for that. They constantly give up pleasures which they consider in no way evil. That requires strength of will. But such strength is the most admired virtue in Japan."

The Ugly Japanese

Malefactors can be as instructive as paragons and probably are more interesting. Some of the main traits of the ugly Japanese stand out clearly in the recent motion picture *Anata Kaimasu*.

The title is given in English as "I'll Buy You," but this hides ambiguities in the original. The original title consists of a neutral second-person singular pronoun, plus the ordinary verb for "to buy." In spoken Japanese the two words together could be pronounced in two different intonation patterns. One of these could be translated as "I'll Buy You," but the other then would translate as "You'll Buy Me." There are still other ambiguities which the translator has to choose among, such that other possible translations could be We'll Buy You, They'll Buy You, You'll Buy Us, or You'll Buy Them.

Expectably enough the film dramatizes the pricing and marketing of selves. The theme is a common one in Western movies too, but in *Anata Kaimasu* it is handled in a distinctive way. The main transaction involves Kurita, who at first glance is a clean-cut college baseball hero, a sort of All Japanese Boy, about to graduate from college and being sought by every major league pro team. However the issue is not so much the pure Kurita versus the evils of human trafficking, as seems usual in American star-is-born films. The marketing of selves is dealt with in a more detached, at times almost clinical, way. To an American social scientist it calls to mind the writings of George Casper Homans on human behavior as exchange.

For Kurita is by no means the only self in the market. Everyone is buying and selling: his guardian, his girl friend, his four elder brothers, and the chorus of fawning, gift-laden professional scouts and managers. The point is less that people play dirty pool in the market than that the market is naturally a dirty pool. This has simply got to be accepted. For example, the girl friend at first is dart-tongued to Kishimoto, the "good" scout through whose eyes the story unfolds. Eventually, however, Kishimoto accuses her of being unrealistic. His actions in the market may seem ugly, but in his soul is beauty. At this she mellows toward him and admits that, yes, a person and the demands of his social position are not one thing but two.

Furthermore, it is not evil to charge what the traffic will bear. Many scenes in the film travesty upon expense-account wooing. Kurita and his friends are lavishly treated at fashionable restaurants and resorts. The scouts come bearing gift tractors to the brothers, airplane tickets to the guardian, suitcases to the girl friend. The implication is that you should feel free to enjoy these things if they come your way, for they are enjoyable. But you must not assume that such presents express genuine human feelings; they usually are social-role performance. They need not be both.

As the scouts begin to descend upon Kurita he diverts them to his guardian. (Before Kurita's father died some years earlier, by written testament he put the boy into the charge of a friend and asked him to see to the boy's future.) The guardian seems to be a rather shady sort, however. He operates a hole-in-the-wall import business. At one point we are told that during the war in China he had been a spy—some say, for the Chinese. He has separated from his wife and child, although he sends them money for support; and he lives openly with another woman. Probably not a man to be trusted.

But he craves personal trust. His first words to the camera are, I detest flattery! In a sense he bought, or tried to buy, Kurita's loyalty by paying the boy's way through college. But he insists that he did so out of human decency and friendship with the boy's father. He anticipated no financial gain from it. If Kurita wishes to return to the farm after graduation, the guardian will never say a word against it. However, if Kurita does intend to turn professional, then he should listen to his guardian, who has had long experience in bargaining, before signing with any team.

Kurita's true ugliness, however, is that he refuses to heed any of those in his nexus. When this becomes unmistakable, the event precipitates a fatal attack of the guardian's gallstones. As word is brought that the guardian is in his last moments, Kurita is announcing his decision to join the Osaka team. He refuses to rush to the guardian's bedside, saying he has his own affairs to attend, for the reporters are begging for interviews. In another scene when the good scout Kishimoto upbraids Kurita for callousness, Kurita replies that it is his life to live as he wants. At this his girl friend slaps his face and screams that he is a coward. He does not have the courage to live out his obligations to those in his nexus.

His family is ruined too. His brothers argued with him that blood is thicker than ink; they are his elders and he should think of their welfare, i.e., choose the team that will pay them the most in benefits for influencing his decision. But when they realize that he has not heeded them either, brother turns upon brother. One stabs another and is taken to jail. Household harmony becomes a shambles. Kurita's selfishness has destroyed the whole nexus. Gone are guardian, girl friend, and brothers. He has had his way. But his way has been *wagamama*, wilfully selfish, literally "the self as it is." And at what a price!

Sympathy

Kurita's crime is compound. Not only is he cowardly, because unwilling to suppress selfish desires out of duty to others; he also is cavalier, because unwilling to show sympathy for their human feelings. He has been stringing them along, encouraging them to believe that he cares for them—and then it becomes clear that his heart is an icicle. It is for this that the good scout Kishimoto upbraids him. If you realized all along, he snaps, that you were going to ignore your friends, the very least you could have done was to tell them from the beginning.

Japanese ideals of sympathy are even more difficult to translate than their ideals of duty. To the extent that their notions of unselfish obligation are likely in Western eyes to seem stifling, their notions of sensitivity to the feelings of others are likely to seem sodden. The unfamiliar always is difficult to categorize. But the West has been too quick to read into Japanese ethics a set of conflicting and irreconcilable opposites: of beauty and beastliness, of chrysanthemums and swords. And Japanese who have tried to explain their own codes have not always helped by striking a tough-but-oh-so-gentle pose that is confusing even when not conceited.

The Japanese ideal not only says that the feelings, thoughts, and reactions of the self are real, even though they must be subordinate to group goals; it also says that these emotions are felt by all selves. This is human nature. The waku presses upon every self—of course upon some more than others—and the good Japanese is the one who can take it. But all selves are feeling selves, and they deserve sympathetic support lest the waku snuff out human feeling. On these grounds we need to add a fourth premise to Pelzel's paradigm:

Four, where group goals are not in danger, the group is oriented toward the human feelings of its members—toward supporting their quest for personal fulfillment.

Sympathy too is an ideal, to be lived out. There are several Japanese terms for it, although in recent times probably the most common is *ninjō*; and in many novels and dramas of the past three centuries the dilemma of virtue is one between ninjō and *giri* ("duty"). Ninjō is not one of those words that can be readily defined, any more than a Western word that it partly overlaps, love. But it does have a focus of meaning, which Pelzel explains in this way: "The idea of *ninjō* seems to me straightforward; it means 'human emotions' of course and by extension 'human nature.' As a proper motivation, it counsels being aware of and reacting sympathetically to the other person as a sentient human being. The emphasis here is upon the word 'sentiment' which seems to be of primary concern: the other person's capacity, in other words, to feel pleasure or pain. Now insofar as one acts in terms of the ideal, one will tend to try to foresee the consequences of action upon the other individual's capacity to feel pleasure and pain, and will modify behavior to maximize the former and forestall the latter."

All those within a nexus should strive to live with sympathy. Neither leader nor follower should demand of the other what is sure to bring unreasonable pain. Marriage offers a good illustration. The Japanese are said to prefer arranged marriage. Observers often interpret this to mean that children are married off according to little more than parental whim. It is true that group goals take priority, and a son may be urged to take a bride for the sake of the family even though he is not personally attracted to her. But the arranging process usually is exceedingly complex, as one can see from Tanizaki's novel, *The Makioka Sisters*. Through repeated family discussions, through the use of go-betweens, through "accidental" meetings arranged for the prospective spouses, there is an attempt to find that solution which will best satisfy both the desires and the obligations of all concerned. The good parent will not crudely force a decision adverse to his child's desires. The good child will recognize that his parents must balance their sympathy for him as person against their responsibility to the nexus as a whole.

In a way sympathy is expected even more of seniors than of juniors. Or perhaps more accurately it is expected even more from a self that is in a position to seriously harm or benefit others—like Kurita. Sympathy is a princely virtue in a twofold sense, writes Nitobe Inazo, "princely among the manifold attributes of a noble spirit; princely as particularly befitting a princely profession." To cite the extreme, the samurai should be the most benevolent of men precisely because he holds the ultimate in power, the right to cut down a lesser man on the spot.

The focus continues to be upon the specific and limited human nexus. One ought to be benevolent, sympathetic toward all men. Indeed benevolent toward all living beings, to the extent that Buddhism enters into consideration; but such feelings easily grow tenuous.

Within the circle of one's significant others, however, any failure to be sympathetic is a sting to conscience. It is on these grounds that we can begin to understand the Japanese penchant for organizing themselves into cliques and politico-familistic groupings. The self can rest assured only when it is assured that the leader's power is both checked by his commitment to group goals and backed by his sympathy for all group members.

Gifts may be offered out of sympathy as well as out of social duties. There are "interested" gifts as well as disinterested ones. One cannot always be sure of the difference, and misunderstandings can be hurtful. If the view of the Japanese is somewhat more clinical toward the disinterested gift—as in *Anata Kaimasu*—it seems more eager for the interested gift that comes from the heart. There is a parallel here with those American salesmen who insist that despite the stereotype of their role as "go-get'em" entrepreneurs, what they truly value about their job is its opportunities for human contact. Therefore, they feel that their ready jokes and little presents are expressions of genuine friendship and not just crass devices to keep contacts warm.

In short, the ideal self must be capable of more than repression and energetic performance, capable of more than submissiveness. It must also be capable of entering into relationships of human feeling and intimacy. And this is another sense in which the ability to melt into the nexus is prized. Drinking parties are a good example of how this is manifested. Traveler after traveler has told how easily the Japanese seem to get drunk. Japanese *machismo* does not include being able to hold one's liquor. The usual explanation is that drinking is a permitted indulgence, that so long as one lives up to one's obligations and drinking does not impair performance of them, one can drink without guilt. This is clearly an important aspect of Japanese drinking. But the Westerner tends to assume that a man ought to be able to drink large amounts. That only after a liberal ingestion of superego solvent can the self be dissolved enough so that it will say what it thinks. Japanese *machismo* by contrast goes out more to the man who becomes drunk easily. To drink and "not crumble" (*kuzurenai*) is to reject an opportunity mutually to offer human sympathy. Such a man, however tough, is never so gentle.

Labor and Leisure

We see, then, that the ideal self is other-directed. But measured against Western ideals it is particularly other-directed along political lines. What its radar is attuned to is the social framework of a limited and specific human nexus. It strives to support the nexus and to further its goals. It enjoys its personal, selfish feelings, thoughts, and reactions but it restrains them when they might be disruptive. And it is sensitive to the human feelings of others.

Applied to questions of the search for enjoyment, this view differs from the Western view in some respects. We can make this clear most easily by contrasting Japanese and Western nuances of various terms.

Labor and frugality do not for Japanese have the sort of "inherent" virtue they do in the West. Man is not condemned to Faustian restlessness, and a penny saved is not automatically a blow against the Tempter. What is ennobling is performance, the self's contributions to group goals. And to the degree that labor and frugality are parts of performance, then they do become ennobling. Performance is, of course, performance of those tasks allocated to one's station (*waku no naka ni waria-taerareta shigoto*). Anything beyond this is supereroga-tion—the opportunity for self-flattery by enduring heavy labor and low wages.

Time is clocked more on a political than a mechanical basis. The Japanese are by no means ignorant of Poor Richard's dictum that time is money, but time counts first of all as time in which to complete group tasks. The West speaks of overtime; the Japanese equivalent *zangyō* is literally "leftover tasks." In practice this cuts several ways. The good employee should not balk at being asked to stay at his desk into the night to complete an assign-ment, nor complain if there is not enough time for him to take a full vacation. But conversely the good employer should have enough feeling for his men that he does not quibble over punctuality nor demand constant attend-ance. Or, again, a university lecturer who wants to be popular with his students will cancel about a third of his scheduled classes, and he usually will not lecture for more than about two-thirds of his allotted two hours per session.

Efficiency, thus, is not open to ready measurement by a Tayloristic calculus of X motions in Y time. (Although the concept is attracting the interest of Japanese man-agers.) One labors with a target in mind, and this may at times include a target cost and target date, but in the last analysis what counts is performing the task regardless of time and cost. A loose parallel, but one that makes the point, is the American crash-program attitude toward any felt threat to national security.

Leisure and consumption are not inherently evil in Japanese eyes; the devil does not make work for idle hands. However, they may become evil if they are not licensed by the nexus, either in terms of one's specific station (e.g. women do not have drinking parties) or in terms of a general holiday. One of the most common words for leisure, *yoka*, connotes "surplus time" or "spare time," the after hours when one is off duty from the nexus. Overactive consumption could endanger diligence, though. Following this line of argument, some Japanese moralists have preached that action (i.e. the motions of daily living) must equate with production, *seikatsu* equal *seisan*. However, relaxation comes relatively easily to most Japanese when off duty. So easily, in fact, that some Japanese critics in recent years have spoken of this as a national disgrace—that too many men are napping when they should be employing their after hours actively. But when one goes off duty there is a sense in which one becomes socially dead. If nothing has to be done, why should one struggle to do anything? This is how I would begin to account for the proverbial Japanese ability to drift asleep at almost any time and place where "nothing" is happening.

The after hours also may be used for personal pursuits. Here I suspect that there is less difference between Japanese and Western ideals than might appear superficially, although there are unmistakable divergences in accent. For one thing, the Western view stresses leisure as an individual affair, and free choice is favored. The Japanese ideal is open to free choice but also less closed to the possibilities of group enjoyment. There are Japanese phrases equivalent to *de gustibus*. Shucking off the nexus and entering into "nature" has long been honored as a personal affair. In this respect many Japanese would second Freud's suggestion that "Voluntary loneliness, isolation from others, is the readiest safeguard against the unhappiness that may arise out of human relations." But there also is a strong penchant for the use of free time in mutual attention to human feeling. For another thing, where the West tends to speak of leisure as a cultivation of the self, the Japanese have tended more to speak of it as the pursuit of selflessness. One takes lessons, in calligraphy, in fencing, dancing—even in golf—not merely to acquire skill. One seeks ultimately the sort of skill that carries one to the "realm of the non-self" where one acts without being aware that "I" am acting. In the after hours as before, the ultimate is a spirit of selflessness.

The Return of the Repressed

It would be naive to think that because a cultural ideal favors certain virtues these are more common in the population. And it would be even more naive to claim that ideals lead directly to a racial, or psychoracial, oversoul. The view we have been sketching is an historic emergent. It has developed from the continuing interplay of many vectors, pressure groups, veto powers, and vested interests. It is the "official" view propagated internally by teachers and leaders, and propagandized externally by cultural ambassadors. It is the view incorporated in those self-objectifying performances where one expresses what it means to be Japanese—as in the uses of Ninomiya Kinjirō.

In the modern epoch this ideal has at times been enforced harshly, but at times there have been moratorium moods when the "hundred flowers" of plural ideals have severally been cultivated. In the early years of the Meiji period Japan was remarkably open (*pace* Perry, more open than opened), and Western notions of many sorts were sampled. However, a wave of reaction set in during the 1890's. In the 1920's, favored by postwar prosperity, the Japanese were caught up in the global groundswell of the first twentieth-century search for enjoyment. In Japan as in the West it was a Fitzgeraldian age of flappers (called *moga*, short for *modan gāru*, "modern girl"), of silent films, and of "contemporary hedonism." (The first Japanese studies of leisure as a social problem date from this period.) After 1936 this was swamped by patriotic righteousness, but now in the postwar years of relative plenty there is renewed attention to life and its joys.

One should avoid overestimating the amount of change. If the Japanese are developing a sort of "fun morality," it does not mean that they have switched from stressing the happiness of duty to stressing only the duty of happiness. We gain some sense of the spread of current attitudes from recent surveys. The table below shows differences in attitudes to work and play among a sample of urban male voters. The study was carried out by the Tokyo University Newspaper Research Institute in 1959 on a total sample (male and female) of 1,200 voters (914 completed interviews) in twenty-three metropolitan Tokyo wards. (Since this is a purely metropolitan sample, it probably underrepresents the strength of Ninomiya-ish attitudes in the nation as a whole.)

(all figures in percentages)	work is a duty (1)	work is work, play is play (2)	work is a joy (4)	rest in order to work (5)	(3), (6), and don't know
by age					
20–29	8.4	50.0	9.0	25.3	7.3
30–39	10.3	51.0	9.0	22.8	6.4
40–49	23.4	30.6	13.5	25.2	7.3
50 and older	34.4	23.2	18.5	10.6	13.5

(all figures in percentages)	work is a duty (1)	work is work, play is play (2)	work is a joy (4)	rest in order to work (5)	(3), (6), and don't know
by occupation					
white collar, large enterprise	13.3	61.3	5.3	10.7	9.4
white collar, small and medium enterprise	15.7	44.3	10.0	27.1	2.9
laborer, large enterprise	15.7	50.0	12.5	15.7	1.1
laborer, small and medium enterprise	15.3	42.7	12.1	25.0	4.9
independent operator.	19.0	30.8	15.4	27.3	7.5
TOTALS	18.8	39.4	12.4	20.9	8.7

Each respondent was asked to choose one of the following statements as best representing his own attitude:

1. Since doing work is a human duty, I must work to the limits of my time.

2. Work is work, play is play. Work diligently during set working hours, and when released from work forget it and play.

3. Work is a means to subsistence. I try to do a suitable amount of it, then as much as possible enjoy myself playing.

4. Work is a form of enjoyment. I haven't especially thought about wanting to be emancipated from work in order to play.

5. I like work, but I need to have enough time for the

rest and relaxation essential to build up my energy for working.

6. There is no point to making drudgery of human life. I think it is good to do what you yourself want to do.

There were so few responses to (3) and (6) that in the table these are combined with "don't know." The majority preference is for what the researchers describe as a "rationalistic" attitude—(2) "work is work, play is play"—in the early years but diminishing with increasing age. However, not a few regard work as a duty (1) or a pleasure (4), especially in the older age ranges. "Rationalistic" attitudes similarly are stronger among workers in large enterprises than among those in smaller enterprises; and especially stronger than among independent operators who, like Mr. Akinai, are much less likely to punch a timecard.

At any event, whatever the future holds, "Ninomiya-ish" has become a *Schimpfwort*. It carries almost as much opprobrium as "feudalistic." There is a saying that to understand what a man is talking about you must understand what he is talking against. Today as the Japanese talk about the after hours one does not always know what they are speaking for, but one cannot mistake what they are speaking against. They are speaking against the assumption that the model is Ninomiya Kinjirō.

5. *The After Hours*

Jehovah, the bearded and angry God, gave his worshippers the supreme example of ideal laziness; after six days of work, He rests for all eternity.   PAUL LAFARGUE

95

Time's Arrows

As the Ninomiya image takes on tarnish, the clock and the calendar take on luster. If the after hours are truly a time of opportunity, then one wants more of them and wants them more clearly demarcated. The Japanese of the nineteen-sixties are telling each other that they prefer a shorter working day, more holidays, longer vacations (with pay), and a more secure retirement. They also are telling each other to be more conscious of the divisions of time.

As in the West, many factors have been operating. It is easier to name them than closely to calculate their respective strengths, but two features especially merit attention. One is the demographic trend in styles of living. Since the twenties, and increasingly since the war, salarymen and other employees of large industrial and commercial concerns are coming to make up an ever larger plurality of the labor force. They—along with all schoolchildren—have become accustomed to regular hours and days at a workplace clearly segregated from their homes. And the regularity of this routine has become attractive to farmers, shopkeepers, and housewives who suffer from what now are regarded as "underprivileged" minority lifestyles.

The other feature is the growing demand for synchronic coördination of human affairs that is so much a part of modern living. In Lewis Mumford's dictum, "The clock, not the steam-engine, is the key-machine of the modern industrial age." This is no slander against the horological acumen of preindustrial mankind. After all, pocket sundials have been unearthed from Imperial Rome, and Roman waterclocks attained remarkable complexity. It was technically possible to adhere to rigid schedules, but probably not often necessary. In a vast industrial civilization this kind of flexibility less easily obtains. The more that labor is divided, the more organization needed to reintegrate it. As Peter Drucker has said, "The mass-production principle is not a mechanical principle. If it were, it could never have been applied beyond manufacturing, and independently of assembly line, conveyor belt and interchangeable parts. It is a *social* principle—a principle of *human* organization. What was new in Ford's plant was not the organization of mechanical forces, but the organization of human beings performing a common task." Untimeliness becomes a luxury.

It is fashionable to boast of the increased free time made available to industrial man. We read again and again that over the past century the average work week in the United States has declined from seventy to forty hours. Some persons speak grandly of the "provoking gift of leisure," a clear proof of human progress. All across the globe the shorter work week has become a target for national aspirations, and in Japan critics indulge in cultural self-flagellation because the domestic work week stands yet at fifty-plus hours.

But if it is fashionable it is also foolish. In our craving for reassurance of betterment we allow a gilded figure to lure our attention from the transformations in the whole ground-tempo of modern daily living. It is possible to cite other equally reliable statistics to indicate that working hours in general have *not* declined radically. Recently both Harold Wilensky and Sebastian de Grazia have done just that as a means to debunking the "illusion" of more free time. However, debunking is beside the point. (Or rather it leads to a different problem, one in the social sources of ideology: Why is it that some people prefer to believe that they have more leisure than their grandfathers?) For whether or not the after hours are very much on the increase—and there does seem to be *some* change—they are very much being distributed according to a different tempo.

The tempo of living felt to be most appropriate to today's industrial Japan was set forth in the labor standards laws of 1947. These laws accord with International Labor Office conventions, but allow for parochial conditions such as company dormitories. Concerning time, the laws prescribe:

A working *day* of eight hours maximum, with a pay premium of at least 25 per cent for overtime. A similar pay premium is required for work between 10:00 P.M. and 5:00 A.M. Women and minors (under eighteen) are not to work at night. There must be at least forty-five minutes of recess during every six to eight hour shift; if the shift exceeds eight hours the recess must be increased to sixty minutes.

A working *week* of six days, again with a 25 per cent premium for holiday employment.

A working *year* with an annual paid vacation, in addition to the fifty-two weekly holidays and women's menstrual leaves. There should be six days of vacation for any employee who has worked regularly for one year; one day of vacation is added for each additional year of employment, up to a maximum of twenty days.

The postwar code is widely acclaimed as an upgrading of public standards, though some of its provisions existed piecemeal before 1947. For example, the eight-hour day was common in some Tokugawa craft guilds, and pensions were provided for some civil servants as early as 1871. But the code collates many of the "best" practices (however it does not provide for a minimum wage) and makes them applicable to a larger bloc of workers. Nevertheless, for the labor force as a whole the code still is more model than modal. The laws are a bamboo basket (*zaru hō*), complain labor spokesmen, since they allow so many holes. And indeed, the basic law applies only to establishments with five or more employees. This encompasses about two-thirds of the industrial workers but omits those in familistic establishments as well as those in agriculture or domestic service. But the years since 1947 have witnessed growing demands that the general pattern be extended to all who labor, down to the last unfortunate apprentice and farm bride. And officials of the regional Labor Standards Offices have been coaxing compliance even from those small employers not legally bound to the code.

For a less passionate perspective upon this "provoking gift" we shall investigate two topics. The first concerns patterns of scheduling: how are the after hours calculated, in terms of days and years, and who has how much of which? This we take up now. The second concerns the uses of these after hours, and this we reserve for the next chapter.

In Chapter 4 I spoke of culture as a set of orientations to experience. The term is also used to mean lifeways and customs, sets of "blueprints" for the conduct of human affairs. One such set in any culture prescribes schedules for action in time, "a structure of timing and progressing for human lives and human relationships," as Conrad Arensberg puts it. In the sections that follow, I sketch some of the regular rounds of modern Japanese life. A sketch of this kind inevitably suffers from vagueness when contrasted with the concrete rounds of the three Anchiku families we visited earlier. However, it must be attempted if we are to comprehend the environment within which groups and individuals work out their temporal life chances.

Sketching these rounds is difficult enough without slipping into the quicksands of endless qualification. Attempting to assay the weight of affect that adheres to each round is a form of sparring with the impossible. On the surface these schedules may seem emotionally bland. They are so much a "given" part of life—like the configurations of the Roman alphabet or the *kana* syllabary—that we rarely stop to wonder about them. They seem to be only means to an end; we wax compulsive about them only to the extent that we favor the comforts of regularity. But they are not irresistible forces. Scripts have been scrapped and calendars changed. Sometimes these "means" become "ends," articulately taken up for propagation, approval, or condemnation. It may be that the "provoking gift" is less due to increased amounts of free time than to an only partly conscious awareness that traditional schedules are out of joint with the times. So as part of our task we must also look into current demands for schedule revision.

The Declining Workday

The idea of a "typical daily round" is a construct, of course; a deliberate simplification. Anyone attuned to the variability of human affairs cannot but want to urge immediate qualifications. After all, the daily round usually refers to workdays, not holidays. It is not quite the same on a Monday as on a Friday even though both be working days. It varies considerably with occupation, from the staccato "mechanical" tempo of the assembly line worker to the longer hours but apparently less demanding pace of the cobbler or the housewife. It usually has some seasonal shifts even for the stereotypic dial watcher, although they may not be as obvious as those enjoyed by the stereotypic fisherman out under the elements. But though it is a construct it is not merely a scholar's device. Ordinary men and women also use it in allocating their energies to the tasks at hand.

Historical information on the daily round is scarce. Apart from polemics on the length of the workday, secondary sources virtually do not exist. From the evidence in hand one can discern notable changes over the past century, although there are also important points of continuity. Most apparent is a greater standardization of schedules and timepieces (with parallels to the history of Standard Time in the West). Tokugawa-era Japan did not lack for timepieces, and Edo is an exception to Gideon Sjoberg's assertion that "Pre-industrial urbanites, even if they wanted to, could not adhere to fixed schedules." Temples and castles announced the hours of the day, and neighborhood watchmen those of the night. Mechanical clocks probably were a plaything of the wealthy, but waterclocks were more widely diffused. And for measuring short intervals anyone could burn knotted cords or sticks of incense. (Geisha fees were calculated per stick of incense.) In Saikaku's novel *A Man Who Loved Love*, a courtesan named Yoshino is praised because she can "play the harp, sing songs, prepare tea; is not dissolute, can arrange flowers, and reset the clepsydra." The latter was no trifling task, for the length of the hour was flexible, varying with the length of daylight, as did the Roman hour. The day was divided into twelve units, but sunrise and sunset always came at the sixth hour, and the intervals between them were regularly subdivided. Since these intervals vary continuously throughout the year, the clock had to be reset every few days. This also means that the working day, for urbanites as well as farmers, waxed and waned with the annual motions of the earth. The system continued in use until 1873, when the equinoctial hour was made standard throughout the year. Then in 1888 clocks across the nation were adjusted to a single national standard time.

Edo castle gates were open from sunrise to sunset, although small doors could be used at other hours. Merchants unshuttered their stores from sunrise until 10:00 P.M. or so, as continues to be common today in family shops. Farmers, too, were nominally at work with the sun and were urged not to be idle after supper but to busy themselves weaving straw bags and sandals. However, they had the benefit of distinct slack and busy seasons. It is not clear what hours the samurai kept, although Mitamura Engyō claims that midmorning to midafternoon (approximately 10.00 A.M. to 2:00 P.M.) was the ordinary business day in the castles and schools.

Then as now, the Japanese were among those peoples of the world who customarily eat three meals a day. The point may seem trivial, but in this, too, the Japanese were "preadapted" to the modern tempo. The same cannot be said, for example, of many African peoples who report serious disturbances when obliged to abandon a customary two-meal day to comply with the three-meal round in colonial schools, offices, and factories. A pattern of having lunch at noon sharp, and snacks or at least tea at midmorning and midafternoon is widespread today in Japan, and it seems to have been common also in Tokugawa times. One of the usual words for snack, "eights" (*oyatsu*) derives from the Tokugawa word for "eighth hour," the time of the midafternoon snack. Japanese laborers and farmers may take a fourth or even a fifth meal in periods of extended heavy labor.

There is evidence that today's industrial worker has a somewhat shorter average working day than did his Meiji grandfather. But there is little evidence that conditions were markedly different for the farmer until the 1950's, or that for the salaryman they have changed at all. In fact, if Mitamura is right, then apparently the salaryman has a longer day than did the samurai. Much has been said of the sweatshops of the late nineteenth century, which in Japan as in the West had infamously long hours and murderous working conditions. But even granting these evils of early capitalist industry, it is not at all clear that they existed for the bulk of the population then still engaged in other pursuits. And by the 1920's even in industry the working day was within the eight to ten hour range. Today eight hours (or even less) are standard for permanent employees covered by the 1947 code. But if one counts in temporary employees (to whom the code may not apply), overtime, and shops not covered by the law, the average rises to somewhat above eight hours. This, plus a fairly widespread six-day workweek, accounts for the fifty-plus hour working week that dismays some observers and labor leaders, who have begun to press for a five-day forty-hour week.

Other pressures also are felt in nonindustrial circles. For example the Labor Standards Offices have been encouraging the small retail shops to adopt a uniform closing hour at 9:00 P.M. Uniform closing is urged, lest any shopkeeper complain that his competitors are staying open to steal his trade. If we may judge from newspaper reports, at least a *pro forma* compliance has been achieved in many regions. However, in Anchiku it is not unusual for the shutters to be hung but with a fifteen-inch gap left open. The determined customer still can enter. Mitamura mentions a similar practice in Edo. There even has been talk of a regular quitting hour for housewives. And an Aomori villager named Saitō Yaichi reaped a moment of national publicity for sowing a "Mamma's Nine O'clock Movement" (*kattcha kuji undō*) by which the lady of the house would be relieved of all duties on the stroke of 9:00 P.M.

Equally important is a clamor for sharper clock consciousness. Partly this is a call for punctuality, partly it is for more explicit scheduling of one's daily activities. Ben Franklin is cited on the monetary value of time, and Japanese are told to imitate what is understood as an acute American time-sense. As a writer in a weekly magazine put it, somewhat hyperbolically, "It's often said of˙ American switchboard operators—that even though conversations are going on, when quitting time comes they clear the switchboard and go home, so exacting are they about time." The label "land of approximate time" may be valid for some Japanese behavioral contexts, although it surely is overgeneral. Public transportation and communications services, radio, and television, exhibit no shoddiness about time. But meetings do not begin on the appointed hour, and rectification of this "evil old custom" is one plank in the Living Reform Movement. For instance, the Kōfu *Yamanashi Nichinichi* for May 23, 1960, reports that leaders in Hiyoshizu village were decorating neighborhood bulletin boards with this poster:

The Same Time Doesn't Come Twice

Let's all conserve time and respect time. One individual's tardiness is a nuisance to everyone, so let's be sure to hew to the hour for all meetings.

I think that skepticism may be justified, for the expectation is well ingrained that meetings will *not* begin on the dot. (It is an "informal time-set" in Edward T. Hall's terms.) Like the use of "ain't" in English, tardiness in Japan is proper in some contexts. To show up punctually is to be "stupidly honest" (*baka shōjiki*) in the eyes of my Ariake neighbors. And for whatever the fact is worth, a recent comparison of "typical dreams" among Japanese and Americans found that nightmares about being late occur significantly fewer times to the Japanese.

It does not seem surprising that there is a longing for clearer benchmarks in the daily round, especially on the part of those who lack the salaryman's or industrial worker's routine. Not that scheduling urges are a postwar phenomenon. One can see them, for instance, in the farm commune portrayed by Yokoi Jikei in his utopian novel of 1907, *The Model Village*. Here work hours are segregated from other intervals, and community bells call the hands to and from the fields. However, the emphasis in the postwar period has shifted; now the argument is that by scheduling one's work one becomes aware of his leisure. The Women's and Minor's Bureau of the Labor Ministry has been in the forefront of the scheduling movement, seconded by the National Friends Association and various reform leaders. The Bureau has staged surveys and publicity campaigns on the topic, and as a theme for the twelfth annual Women's Week in 1960 it chose "Independent Scheduling of Free Time." The theme was discussed by women's study groups and assemblies across the nation, and the women's pages joined in with anti-Parkinson suggestions. The following sample is from a longer piece on "Ways for a Wife to Make Free Time—Once Again Reconsider Living

Habits," *Chūgoku Shimbun*, Hiroshima, January 23, 1961.

Even though it's called housework time, there are wives who use that time in a jumbled way. It isn't very easy to mark things off, but really, according to the user's way of thinking about them you have days when the 24 hours slip by dreamily, and days when it's possible to live up to a plan. What are the divisions in everyday living time? How many minutes are used for what? Let's look at an example.

If housework isn't jumbled; if you put your mind to it, that's how you can build your family culture. With home electrification and clever contriving you'll find breathing space in your hours and your attitudes; with it you can move toward a daily life of enjoying flower arranging, room decorating, *recreation*, reading, dressing up, and visiting. . . .

The first step in skillfully using time is to chronologically record the activities of the day's 24 hours. It is good to decide and write your plan in the evening for the next day. That way you'll be able to see where you were mistaken and where you were wasteful.

Today she lolled away the whole day. Yesterday was the same, just existing; isn't that pointless? Just leave that kind of wife behind you!

Say what you will, "so busy I've no time to spare" is a demonstration of lack of wisdom. And as for the various obstacles that exist, it takes a wife's courage and resolution to remove them.

Reform leaders have been somewhat less finicky, and have shown more interest in the simpler, familiar Western notion (credited as far back as Alfred the Great) of eight hours' work, eight hours' sleep, and eight hours for fun.

And the Rising Sunday

Scheduling changes have been more obvious in the weekly-to-monthly range. In fact, the seven-day week and its allied concept of a weekly holiday were virtually unknown in Tokugawa Japan. Short-term intervals of workdays and holidays existed, but they were calculated by other methods. Two methods seem to have been most widespread, one making use of the East Asian sexagesimal cycle and the other of the lunisolar month.

The sexagesimal cycle, Sinitic in origin, consists of "ten stems" and "twelve branches" which permutate in a round of sixty units. In theory one could use these to compute a regular interval of any length. In practice intervals of five or ten days were the most common. The cycle was used for such things as planning duty days and liberty days for castle guards, and it was the standard means for calculating market weeks. The cycle lost most of these functions after the Gregorian calendar was adopted early in the Meiji period. However it still is printed on some calendars and almanacs, and one can find a few behavioral survivals such as the "bird-day markets" (*tori no ichi*)—now mainly tourist attractions—in some parts of Tokyo on the "bird" days of the eleventh moon.

The lunisolar calendar was the national standard until 1873. It, too, continues to be included in almanacs and some calendars, but it is little used outside of fishing communities. It consists of alternating months of twenty-nine and thirty days, with a leap-month intercalated seven times every nineteen years to reconcile the disparity between lunar and solar cycles. It was customarily used in three ways for calculating holidays.

The first way was to divide the month into halves. Craftsmen in Tokugawa times, vacated their shops and trades on the first and the fifteenth or sixteenth days of the moon. Matsumoto tailors today continue the practice, although now the Gregorian month is used.

The second way involves a "day numeral." A number from one to nine is chosen and a holiday scheduled for each day on which this number falls: e.g., the eighth, eighteenth, and twenty-eighth days. This generates a work "week" (more accurately, a "decade") of ten days. Decades also survive in some occupations, such as that of Mr. Akinai and his fellow retail grocers in Matsumoto, but here too the Gregorian month now is the basis for calculations.

The third way is to designate one or more specific days of every moon, regardless of interval. Engelbert Kaempfer, resident physician at the Dutch station in Nagasaki harbor in the late seventeenth century, recorded holidays on the first, fifteenth, and twenty-eighth days. In 1960 the two dozen shops affiliated with the Ariake Commercial Association closed their doors on the thirteenth of the month (the general Hotaka Town business holiday) except in January and August. In January and August they closed on the sixteenth, a traditional servants' and apprentices' holiday known as *yabu-iri*.

The Meiji administration adopted the Gregorian calendar in 1873, and declared Sunday a public holiday in 1876. At first, Sunday was taken as a holiday only in government offices, in schools, and in some of the new factories. Since then, however, the weekly holiday has spread widely, and the seven-day week has become one of the most common bases for scheduling events. By the end of the Pacific War, two generations had come to adulthood in a Japan where on Sunday the banks, schools, government offices, and many factories were closed. By that time at least one generation had come of age in a world of commercial radio with its weekly programming. And even the military tacticians demonstrated that they, too, had learned their ethnographic lesson, when they launched an attack upon the American at his most predictable low, 7:00 A.M. on a Sunday morning at Pearl Harbor.

After the war came the firsthand example of Occupation personnel conspicuously consuming their leisure on weekends, and legislating a weekly holiday as part of the 1947 codes. Television has reinforced the weekly broadcasting round; weekly magazines are having an unprecedented boom; even Buddhist groups have experimented with Sunday schools; commemorative weeks clutter the calendar (Human Rights Week, Women's Week, and so on); and the idea of a weekly holiday has caught the eyes of all who toil for a living.

There is no way to estimate the distribution of short-term holidays in the Tokugawa period. Craftsmen seem to have had regular holidays two or three times a month, in addition to annual holidays and seasonal fluctuations. The first and the fifteenth were holidays in some communities, rural as well as urban. The twenty-third night was often used for a regular moon watch, although work may have continued as usual during the day. But on the whole, people seem to have been attuned primarily to the annual round.

At present the weekly holiday is distributed along much the same lines as the eight-hour day—to salarymen, technicians, schoolchildren, and the like. An Economic Planning Board survey of a sample of urban heads of household in 1960 found that slightly more than a third of them had at least one regular day off per week. (However, less than one per cent had two-day weekends—Saturday morning still is for business.) Slightly less than another third had one-to-three holidays per month; the rest reported no fixed holidays in the weekly or monthly range. This and other recent surveys also indicate that two-thirds of the workers in commercial and industrial enterprises have a weekly holiday, but only one-third in wholesale and retail trades. Furthermore, employees of large establishments fare better in this regard than do those in small shops. For example, of shops with more than 30 employees, 80 per cent have a weekly holiday; but of shops with less than four employees, only 20 per cent.

In addition to the weekly holiday the seven-day week has taken root. The Westerner is unthinkingly aware that the days of his weeks have palpably different qualities: Saturday night is the loneliest night, Monday is wash day, Friday is fish day. Suicides are more common on Monday and Tuesday, traffic deaths on Saturday and Sunday. The International Labor Office seems to regard the seven-day week as valid for global statistical purposes, even though weeks of five or ten days are standard in some parts of the world. American brides are given sets of seven dishtowels, each printed or embroidered with the name of one of the days of the week. The model differs in its particulars from class to class, from country to country, from craft to craft. But it governs so many activities that it throws serious blocks in the path of him who would follow a "deviant" schedule. Even the Soviet Union has retreated from post-Revolution attempts to install a five-day week. In Japan, present pressures for extending the weekly holiday system are themselves, I believe, evidence of the extent to which the weekly regimen guides ordinary living. The Japanese have not attained the daily dishtowel stage yet, but the trend is obvious.

Like the eight-hour day or uniform early closing, the weekly holiday is being extended to many in non-industrial occupations. Barbershops in Ariake are closed on Monday; the producers' coöperative on Sunday. In this regard, too, a host of organizations are active: the Labor Standards Offices and Merchants' Associations in urban areas; and in the villages the Women's Clubs and Youth Groups. Where they meet resistance to instituting a weekly holiday, they usually are able to obtain uniform shop closing, or farm holidays twice or thrice per month. Farm holidays (as distinct from festivals or celebrations) are not new in the villages. Even before the war, according to one study, about three-fourths of the 150,000 hamlets (*shūraku*) in the nation had some form of "rest day." However these typically occurred once a month. In 1961, according to an Economic Planning Board survey of 2,169 farm families, about one-third had a farm holiday, frequency per month not specified. This might indicate a postwar decline, but I am not sure that the two studies are comparable.

As we have seen, postwar improvements in farm techniques have leveled all but one or two peaks in the curve of labor demand over the growing season. The farmer presumably could take one day off in seven if he chose, although he more commonly prefers to take on wage labor in a factory or store and leave the routine farm tasks to his wife. But the farm house head regularly employed elsewhere also is more likely to have a regular day off from his employment. This is reflected in the Economic Planning Board Survey. The percentage of fixed rest days show a rise from house heads who only farm (30.3 per cent) to those who mainly farm but have secondary occupations (35.2 per cent) to those who farm merely as a sideline (38.4 per cent).

Opinion leaders have done their part by contributing justifications for weekly holidays. They argue that regularity leads to greater efficiency through "proper" leisure. Take for example the following piece by Shimizu Aki, Professor of Business at Meiji University, from the *San'yō Shimbun*, Okayama, of September 14, 1960. Shimizu tells of a Shikoku greengrocer who is the epitome of capitalist diligence, but who is frustrated because his clerks are continually taking time off. He can't do much about it, either, because these days a good clerk is hard to find. However, in that Shikoku town almost every shopping street observes uniform closing twice a month, whereas this greengrocer never takes a holiday. Naturally the clerks are always finding excuses for not working:

> Really it is just because this shop owner is a super-humanly powerful type that he is able to go on year-round without a holiday. For that very reason it is not proper for him to force this on all the clerks. Regardless of the provisions of the Labor Standards Laws, this isn't the way to a real increase in efficiency. In rest periods stick to resting—this is the way to a real increase in efficiency. In this age when you have to use your head in business, young clerks can't merely follow the path of an eternally Ninomiya Kinjirō-ish "denial and diligence," and they don't follow it. He ought to regard his clerks' taking time off more as a necessary and legitimate self-defense.

The argument for regularity has a long pedigree. When one of Confucius' disciples was puzzled by festival riotousness, the Master said that even Wen and Wu, the heroic emperors of the golden age, "could not keep a bow in good condition if it were always drawn and never relaxed; nor did they leave it always relaxed and never drawn. To keep it now strung and now unstrung was the way of Wen and Wu." At least one late Tokugawa scholar was even more to the point. Suzuki Masayuki, a "national studies scholar" (*kokugakusha*) from Ibaraki, argued that "In agriculture if there are too few holidays this naturally breeds negligence, so one ought to set a half-holiday every sixth or seventh day. If there is a fixed holiday, then as has long been hoped for, there will be no carelessness at work, and efficiency will rise such that even in a half day one full day's work can be done." The same line is taken today to justify a two-day weekend. As an editorial writer put it in the *Asahi Evening News* for January 13, 1961:

> The salaryman probably wants to lie down on the one day he gets off each week. This does not necessarily suit his wife and children, who spend most of their time at home. If the whole family goes out for recreation, the salaryman's weariness is increased by the crowds in the trains. This explains the "Monday morning feeling" that salary earners suffer from.
>
> People in the United States and Britain have two days off a week. One day is spent resting and the other is devoted to social activities. If a person has only one day off a week, he will become exhausted if he is too energetic that day.

Captains of labor predictably enough favor a two-day weekend, and so do some captains of industry. In a much-publicized speech, Matsushita Kōnosuke, president of Matsushita Electric, told his employees that by 1965 the company must develop a two-day weekend. Trade liberalization places the company in direct competition with foreign as well as domestic producers; greater efficiency is inescapable. Part of it can be accomplished by technological improvements, but the rest must come from improved human output.

So if you ask me why, it is because every day will become an extremely busy one, and even phone calls that until now have been made casually no longer can be made casually. If the call took three minutes, finish it in one; and furthermore, practice concluding business smartly. The same goes for production in the shop. . . . With the company that highly rationalized, it means we work with our machines without so much as a side glance; and half to restore weariness from it we rest on Saturday, half to enjoy a higher standard of living we take a holiday on Sunday. . . .

Weekly regularity, then, is said to improve both the working hours and the after hours. The latter stress can be glimpsed from the following excerpt from a prize essay selected by the Tochigi Prefecture Labor Standards Office in October, 1960, in a contest on "The Weekly Holiday System and the Proper Use of Leisure."

The winner first explains that she works in a small wholesale shop dealing in ready-made clothes. The shop used to close twice a month, but in those days, by the second week after the holiday all the girls would begin to drop out because of exhaustion.

When there are two holidays a month, even though you plan to use them effectively, as each holiday comes around it is as though there is no place to settle, you are completely exhausted, you don't do anything, you can't do anything; and you end up indulging in a nap to ease your weariness. To me "Proper Use of Leisure" was so distant a thing I couldn't even think about it. However, since February of this year we have had a weekly holiday system, and it has made it possible for us to pass the days composed and satisfied in body and soul. . . .

Furthermore we workers have come to be able to use our Sunday leisure profitably. We read books to better our education, we participate in meetings to improve our social awareness; our enthusiasm and will to work increases, and the cumulative fatigue of overexertion has disappeared. We realize how the weekly holiday system gives birth to good results and how it can favor the general development of society.

The less enchanted observer may well wonder what magic there is in the number seven. Admitting the virtues of regularity, couldn't a holiday every sixth or ninth day do as well? The obvious implication is that while regularity may be rational, the sabbath regime is arbitrary. Hutton Webster long ago pointed out in his *Rest Days* that all known seven day weeks can be traced to an origin in the ancient Middle East. Like the alphabet, the sabbath has been one of the Middle East's contributions to world civilization.

Perhaps *because* it combines arbitrariness with vital functions of standardization, the sabbath regime demands justification. Whether the rationale be sacred or secular matters little from society's point of view. In the West the rationale has mainly been religious, but with secular footnotes. In Japan the rationale is openly secular and "scientific." In both it usually is added that regularity counts for even more under modern conditions, where the "natural" rhythms of physical labor have been supplanted by the "artificial" ones of industry which induce undue mental strain. The ironies of this secularized sabbath have not entirely escaped the Japanese. As an editorial writer twitted in the Sendai *Kahoku Shimpō*, November 17, 1959, "Christian or not, laborers should not be without one holiday a week. To such unfortunate employees we want as soon as possible to spread the Gospel of the weekly holiday."

The Shifting Seasons

A sensitivity to the seasons often is cited as a Japanese peculiarity. Cultural ambassadors pridefully point to practices such as including a seasonal allusion in every haiku, preparing classical paintings in seasonal sets, adding a seasonal greeting to personal correspondence, celebrating seasonal festivals, or sending and seeking each season's first fruits. Japanese of an artistic bent mourn the demise of seasonality in the twentieth century; they say its softer melodies cannot be heard above the jazz downbeat of modernity. Tanizaki writes in 1934 of how electricity has dimmed the autumn moon:

> The day before the full moon, however, I read in the paper that there would be loudspeakers in the woods at Ishiyama to regale the moon-viewing guests with phonograph records of the Moonlight Sonata. I cancelled my plans immediately. Loudspeakers were bad enough, but if it could be assumed that they would set the tone, then there would surely be floodlights strung all over the mountain. I remember another ruined moon-viewing, the year we took a boat on the night of the harvest full moon and sailed out over the lake of the Suma Temple. We put together a party, we had our refreshments in lacquered boxes, we set bravely out. But the margin of the lake was decorated brilliantly with electric lights in five colors. There was indeed a moon if one strained one's eyes for it.

But to stop there is to leave half the song unsung. Jazz, too, has its rhythms and its melodic progressions, and so does the modern annual round. The Japanese calendar has come to include an array of new annual events, such as days for Mother, Constitution, Christmas, and Culture. And it orchestrates an array of new seasons—however loosely linked to meteorological nature —such as those for professional baseball, school vacations, or the annual exodus to the ski slopes. We could as readily trace the modernization of Matsumoto in calendar time as in town-plan space. The point is not to mourn the loss of seasonality but to realize that it has been transformed.

The calendar, in Durkheim's famous epigram, "expresses the rhythm of the collective activities, while at the same time its function is to assure their regularity." This refers to the calendar of *events*, not to the abstract device hung on the wall. The distinction is essential, for Japanese folklorists like to blame the Meiji administration for ruining the traditional cycle of annual events by importing the Gregorian calendar. The latter, they say, is not so well suited to the seasons as is the lunisolar reckoning. This puts the blame erroneously. If anything the Gregorian calendar is better suited to annual seasonal swings, in that it more closely correlates with solar changes. The real villains are otherwise: first, the lunisolar calendar had an associated complex of *events* that were adapted to seasonality, and these had to be recalibrated according to Gregorian reckoning; second, while this was taking place, the currents of modernization were carrying in new seasons and events and sweeping away many of the old.

After 1873 national public holidays were celebrated by the Gregorian scheme and made uniform throughout the empire. Popular holidays, however, underwent a shuffling whose traces still survive. For example some communities (25 per cent according to one postwar survey) still celebrate New Year's by the old calendar. Usually this is in addition to a New Year's celebration on Gregorian January 1. This doubling of holidays is a luxury which the New Living Movement leaders brand as "irrational" and the Ministry of Education as "superstitious." In still other communities (four per cent of the same survey) the New Year is celebrated by Gregorian reckoning, but one month late. This is an attempt to preserve seasonal connotations, since holidays under the old calendar tended to occur a few weeks later vis-à-vis the seasons than they do by Gregorian calculus. In Anchiku most people observe New Year's on Gregorian January 1, but they celebrate four other events by the month-late system: Girls' Day, Boys' Day, Tanabata, and Bon.

The Tokugawa administration vacated its offices on the Five Breaks, plus New Year's, Midsummer, June 6 (*Kajō*), and August 1 (*Hassaku*); this was imitated in most of the provinces. The Meiji government replaced this list with a nation-and-emperor centered one in 1873; and despite vicissitudes the official public roster has continued to range between eight and twelve annual events, presently standing at nine.

Folklorists have recorded regional and local variations in folk festivals and annual events with narcissistic attention to "local color." It is possible to trace changes over the century accurately for individual communities, but impossible to generalize confidently for the nation. For most communities, despite ups and downs, the total number of events remains in the thirty-to-forty range. However a mere count is not very revealing, since some holidays require elaborate preparation, whereas others may involve no more than adding a special dish to the evening meal. Furthermore, one finds great variation from house to house, depending on location, occupation, family preferences, or stage in the family cycle.

Recent opinion on the annual round, like that on the day and week, favors more holidays and more regularity. When the government in 1960 announced a ten-year plan for doubling the national income, a Liberal-Democrat faction under Kōno Ichirō introduced a bill for trebling the national holidays. The Socialists and Social Democrats first yelled Publicity Stunt!—but then drafted similar proposals of their own. The Kōno bill would provide 26 holidays in all. The first day of each month would become a People's Rest Day (except New Year's Day, which already is a holiday). The present nine holidays would be retained: New Year's, Adults' Day (January 15), Vernal Equinox (March 21 or 22), Emperor's Birthday (April 29), Constitution Day (May 3), Children's Day (May 5), Autumnal Equinox (September 23 or 24), Culture Day (November 3), and Labor Thanksgiving Day (November 23). And six new days would be added, one for each of the months now holiday-underprivileged: National Foundation Day (February 11), Old People's Day (June 10), Obon Day (July 15), Peace Day (August 15), Sports Day (October 10), and International Goodwill Day (December 25).

Apart from day-wage workers and small entrepreneurs, no one seemed opposed to an increase; but many people were critical, even incredulous, of some of the suggested new days. Would designating Christmas as an International Goodwill Day seem like goodwill to most Africans and Asians? Peace Day is a noble thought, but to suggest celebrating peace on the anniversary of the Pacific War surrender was bad form, to put it mildly. And though most nation-states have a Foundation Day, to suggest this on the date of *Kigensetsu*, the prewar Empire Day with its stench of the military and the police state, was an open call to violence. The minority parties stated flatly that *Kigensetsu* under any name still smelled of *Kigensetsu*. And even Prince Mikasa, brother to the Emperor, was reported to have visited Liberal-Democrat offices to register protest in person. A number of writers urged Kōno to abandon the whole proposal. For one thing, they argued, very few of the events seemed worth the trouble. For another thing, because of irregularities between the Gregorian calendar and the seven-day week, holidays sometimes fall on Sunday. Furthermore, even the revised list would have only two holidays in August, when most people want them, and would not eliminate the current mess of "stepping-stone" holidays during "golden week" from April 29 through May 3 and 5. A few voices recommended adopting the "perpetual cal-endar" sometimes discussed in the United Nations—which would have twenty-six working days every month and all annual holidays on Monday. Others suggested discarding all annual holidays in favor of furnishing everyone with a two-day weekend every week. And on a more practical plane several large corporations an-nounced that hereafter they will operate as usual during "golden week" but in compensation will close down for a full week in August. One salaryman encapsuled national opinion when he wrote to the editor of the *Mainichi Shimbun*, April 11, 1960:

> The Golden Week from the end of this month to May 5th is utterly useless, and the fuel losses and such in factories with boilers are uneconomical. There are schemes for transferring holidays, but they just become bargaining issues in union activity or even sources of dis-pute. . . . I earnestly wish that instead of imitating for-

eign countries the Socialists, Social-Democrats, and of course the Conservatives and the government, would coöperate in realizing as soon as possible a meaningfully Japanese set of holidays.

The Coördination Problem

We could expand this sketch to include the life cycle as well. As in the West, Japanese of today go to school longer, take up their trades later, and savor a longer retirement, than their nineteenth-century grandfathers. Education is compulsory through ninth grade; and the 1947 labor codes forbid work by those under sixteen years of age. The codes also provide an array of safeguards for shop conditions, sick leave and health insurance, accident compensation, unemployment aid, and pensions. Japan too is grappling with the problem of angry young men—and angry old ones—both feeling themselves blocked from effective social participation. But this would introduce still further dimensions into an inquiry which for compactness' sake I prefer to limit to the milieu of the ordinary active adult.

I have not argued for a radical change in the *amount* of after hours available to the ordinary active adult. But I have tried to show that over the past century these hours have taken on a different configuration. The change has been greater in some occupations than others, but none has been left untouched. All are falling into step with the regimen typified by the salaryman. We may mourn this kind of homogenization; we probably can do little to prevent it. No doubt it has some built-in limits. With so many humans moving on the same schedule, urban rush-hour sees more mayhem than a Roman circus, and city planners have begun to realize that planning involves time as well as space. Conversely, with so many people seeking entertainment at the same time, facilities quickly become overtaxed. Staggered working hours and staggered vacations are coming to be a public issue. For example, the Sony Corporation shifted its weekly holiday from Sunday to Monday in August, since its employees complained of overcrowded parks on summer Sundays.

It may be that further mechanization and automation will eventually allow greater flexibility in living schedules, as has happened for the farmer. However, increasing automation, whether mechanical in the factories or social in the service trades (e.g., more restaurants or hospitals that never close) will come at the cost of requiring part of the labor force to accept "minority" living schedules. They will work nights and holidays when others around them are at play; they will seek enjoyment when most of their fellows are at work. The problem already is real enough for some occupations, as illustrated by the following letter to the *Tokyo Shimbun*:

> It is contradictory that mailmen should work on Jan. 1. The average person can warm himself at a stove or "kotatsu" and enjoy himself with New Year's food. However, mailmen have to work on such a day, carrying a heavy bag full of New Year's cards.
>
> The Postal Ministry may say that it is delivering cards on the first day of the year as a public service. But this service is at the sacrifice of the mailmen. All Government employees should work on Jan. 1 if mailmen have to work. If it is impossible for Government employees to work on that day, the delivery service should be stopped so that post office workers can take one day off on the first day of the year.

122

At the same time, I urge the public to get rid of such a selfish desire as to wish to receive New Year's cards on the first day of the year. New Year's cards are not directly related to safety of people's lives.

And as phenomena such as the "Sunday neurosis" and "vacation neurosis" warn us, there is more to the enjoyment of the after hours than the mere absence of an obligation to work.

6. *And the Search for Enjoyment*

It is observable in general, that their Festivals and Holidays are days sacred rather to mutual compliments and civilities, than to acts of holiness and devotion, for which reason also they call them Rebi's, which implies as much as Visiting-days. 'Tis true, indeed, that they think it a duty incumbent on them on those days, to go to the Temple of Tensio Daisin, the first and principal object of their worship, and the Temples of their other Gods and deceased great men. And although they are scrupulous enough in the observance of this duty, yet the best part of their time is spent with visiting and complimenting their superiors, friends, and relations.

ENGELBERT KAEMPFER, *The History of Japan* [1690–92]

A Search for Traditions

Just as the earlier Japan had a "structure of timing" for the after hours, so it had guidelines for using them. The Ninomiya image notwithstanding, Tokugawa Japan was well supplied with reasons for *not* working and with ways to go about it. For all his moralizing against the regime, even Sir George Sansom conceded that during the Genroku Era at least (late seventeenth century), the Japanese knew "peace and plenty and a great flourishing of the arts—a happy society as human societies go." This "happy society" had both its high arts and its humble ones—both its kabuki and *senryū*, which are well recorded, and its ordinary "mutual compliments and civilities," which we are able to glimpse through the eyes of that Genroku participant-observer Engelbert Kaempfer. Upon these arts of living, a century of modernization has heaped the outpourings of industrial mass production and marketing. Few of the older ways have completely disappeared, though many, like kabuki, live on in self-conscious classicism. Some, like championship sumō, are now available to almost the entire populace thanks to cheap transport and telecommunications. And all exist in a milieu filled with new ways and means, from television to baseball to the "stand bar." In such a milieu, custom is not always king.

We are likely to overstress the compulsive side of custom and slight the creative. Frazer's generation was fascinated by "survivals" and how they attest the weight of the heavy hand of the past. But we are coming little by little to see and to say that man-in-milieu does not sheepishly "follow" tradition so much as continually *relive* it. After all, if we take the word literally, survivals are items that have "lived across." Even the most traditionalistic of peoples finds itself capable of discarding customs that have lost their savor, and in the modern milieu they may find this inescapable. As Milton Singer puts it, "Their cultural traditions have become problematic hypotheses in an inquiry into the design for a meaningful and worthwhile life." I believe it better to look at this in terms of language. Rare is the man who can radically alter his mother tongue and still make sense. But everywhere are men who continually adapt words, grammar, and rhetoric to the deeds of new days. As they go about it they coin new forms, add nuances to old, or drop them, or borrow notions from elsewhere. All of these processes have occurred in the changing grammar of Japanese systems for scheduling the after hours.' We shall meet them again in the changing rhetorics of Japanese enjoyment.

On the other hand we are likely to understress the compulsive side of the after hours. It is tempting to equate the after hours as an interval to leisure as a quality of living; sometimes the equation also includes freedom as a moral good. "Leisure," writes Kyoto University professor Yoshida Mitsukuni, trying to explain this newly imported Western word, "is time that can be used at free discretion purely on one's own personal affairs." Yoshida is in good company East and West; many use a similar equation. "Leisure time by definition is free time," asserts a U.S. government report. "Any sense of obligation other than what one's tastes and interests invite is a denial of the very essence of leisure." The notion is triply appealing. First, it adds frosting to the cake of progress. If our after hours are "free," then industrialism has made us better off not only naterially but morally too, and our freedom advances

126

with each minute lopped from the working day. Second, it is good Platonism. If men can but be taught their "true" interests—usually coterminous with the author's —then they will not think of wasting their freedom on the false. Education is salvation. Third, the cultural critic discovers that he has boundless scope to cry up his wilderness. With smug logic he can denounce any activity that does not invite his tastes and interests, from cabarets to kabuki, from hiking to haiku.

Tastes and interests are not a trivial matter; the problem is made trivial by being posed only in terms of them. It sets up the after hours as a sort of last oasis for the noble savage struggling through Sapir's "desert patch of merely economic effort." He has only to enter the oasis and be freed. At best this encourages shrugs and cynicism, for where in the world of men and women is any span of time so uncomplicated? Who of us can lightly dismiss in the name of taste or preference the claims of kin, kith, neighbors, or even the importuning advertisers? And if any or every uninvited obligation can be ignored, how then would leisure differ from rampant hedonism, or anomie, or for that matter from catalepsy? A thoroughgoing hedonism, as has often been pointed out, ought to include a rationale for suicide.

At worst the equation entirely avoids the struggles of the self within what A. Irving Hallowell calls its "behavioral environment." Few men, even having attained the oasis, can simply and easily slough off the garments of the journey. This probably is not often pathological, although psychiatrists have names for "leisure neuroses" in men morbidly incapable of even momentarily abandoning their workaday worries. But most of us are well enough enculturated that we need more than mere permission to change what we are doing: we crave directions as to how to go about it. One does not have to envision men as cultural puppets to be able to agree with Bronislaw Malinowski that at times enjoyment actually has to be forced upon people. We may not usually think of it in these terms. None the less, writes Malinowski, in the Trobriand Islands, and *mutatis mutandis* elsewhere: "In almost all tribal enjoyments and festive entertainments on a big scale the same principle obtains. The master of the festivities, by an initial distribution of food, imposes an obligation on the others, to carry through dancing, sports, or games of the season. And indeed, considering the ease with which native enthusiasms flag, with which jealousies, envies and quarrels creep in, and destroy the unanimity of social amusements, the need for compulsion from without to amuse oneself appears not so preposterous as at first sight."

Tastes and interests may be infinitely variable; the modern behavioral environment is not. Living within it, we must adapt to it. The search for enjoyment becomes a search for meaningful and worthwhile guidelines within it. The search is not some simple craving for personal or social paroxysm, though that may be a part of it. It is a search for forms of play that an adult can take seriously. It is a continuing search for traditions.

Out of this search, which encompasses both past-as-known and future-as-expected within the present milieu, people develop styles of living and subcultures of custom. In Chapter 2 we examined the process in the context of families moved by different occupational rhythms. Now let us examine it in the context of the ranges of timing sketched in Chapter 5.

Time's Uses and Abuses

Any frame of reference has its defects, and those of time need to be pointed out, for they are not always evident. In recent decades many investigators have gone about asking people what they "do" with their after hours. The argument seems to be that "leisure" is vague but time concrete; you can trust people to tell how many hours a week they spend on the tennis court or before the TV. Japanese advertisers, media executives, investors, and government planners seem as hungry for this kind of information as do those across the Pacific; and the reports are plentiful. Possibly the planner or advertiser cares to know nothing more than that he has a potential audience of N million on H hour of D day. Surely, just as figures on industrial output help us establish gross national product, so these surveys help us establish gross national preferences. But they tend to draw us away from the milieu rather than toward it, since they proceed by piling abstraction upon abstraction. All investigations suffer from misplaced concreteness. But quantitative surveys of time-use compound this by reducing all activities to a single denominator. "By using a strictly quantitative assembly-line conception of time—time as a moving belt of equal units —one ignores the significance of much activity," writes Sebastian de Grazia. "A moment of awe in religion or ecstasy in love or orgasm in intercourse, a decisive blow to an enemy, relief in a sneeze, or death in a fall is treated as equal to a moment of riding in the bus, shoveling coal, or eating beans. As a matter of fact in most research the former moments get left out altogether."

129

Moreover, any study of time, quantitative or otherwise, tends to be biased in favor of activity. We can readily describe and discuss an explicitly organized event such as a baseball game, but find it more troublesome to conceptualize cocktail conversation even though it may be no less subject to sanctions. We have many words for dividing the stream of activity, but too few for dividing the stream of consciousness.

Furthermore, since discussion has to be discursive it tends to portray people as rather single-minded creatures. Perhaps, as Edward T. Hall has asserted, men in some cultures are more "monochronic" than in others, more given to concentrating upon one thing at a time. But the human stuff everywhere seems to have a vast potential for being "polychronic"; and the stereotypic teenager simultaneously telephoning a friend, watching TV, eating popcorn, and leafing through a comic book is only a limiting case. In Anchiku as in America one finds barbershops and barnyards where work, conversation, and the baseball broadcast take place at the same time. And there are more piquant examples such as my physician-poet landlord, who composes *waka* as he goes his rounds on a motorscooter. One Japanese author has argued that such "whilers" (*nagara-zoku*, people who do one thing while doing another) are well adapted to the modern milieu. "Whiling," writes Tanikawa Shuntarō, has long been morally suspect.

> My mother won't much trust a workman who smokes cigarettes while he's working. At a time when you're working you should devote yourself to the work alone; you can smoke when you take a break—that's her way of thinking about it. In short, try to do two things at once and one of them is sure to come to naught. For my mother this is only common sense.

But in an age when mood music is piped to stores and workshops, it would be absurd to try to listen in academic concentration, head on arms and eyes closed. One has to develop a way of listening while doing other activities.

> For example, it is night and you are sitting alone at your desk with a textbook open. And you try to concentrate on your lessons, but the aftermath of modern daily life with its many stimuli is whirling around you even now when you are alone, and you just can't settle down. . . . So you switch on the radio, and without seeming to listen you begin to hear the late-late jazz program. And then the rhythm of the music appropriately puts a part of your self to sleep and banishes excessive worry and longing; and riding to its pace as though mounted on a belt-conveyor, your studies begin to advance a little as though they were automated.

Probably only in drama or in a first-rate novel can this kind of complexity be conveyed adequately. But it has to be kept in mind in reading what follows.

The length of an interval and the frequency of its recurrence set broad limits to what can be accomplished during it; social and cultural regularities further curb the scope. Even so, a vast array of possibilities remains; I can do no more than suggest central tendencies and offer Anchiku examples. The examples are not more "typically" Japanese than, say, kabuki, karate, or Kurosawa movies. But neither are they less, since no single example can convey the full range of Japaneseness, although all partake of it to some degree. However, in their ordinariness the examples *are* more typical of Anchiku than many of the items from the classical great tradition.

Buakansu

Linguistic fashions are revealing. In 1963 the Japanese began familiarizing themselves with the French word *vacance*, "vacation." (Some say preferred spelling is *buakansu*; the alternative *bakansu* sounds too much like *baka ni su*, "make an ass of.") Vacations in this sense are a product of the modern era, but for centuries the Japanese have taken vacations under other rubrics, especially those of religion and recuperation.

Under religion, records exist from the eighth century onward telling of annual leaves granted to high officials to attend the tutelary festivals of their home communities. The lives of lesser men are not so well documented, but we know that it has long been customary to allow servants, apprentices, and brides to return home for a day or two during New Year's and Midsummer, and occasionally for other festivals. For more than a thousand years pilgrimages to the great temples and shrines have been common even among common folk. Organizations with the suffix -*kō* still exist in many communities. Usually they bear the name of a famous religious center (*Ise-kō*, *Suwa-kō*, etc.) and every year they send thither a delegation to make offerings and bring back talismans.

Under the rubric of recuperation, ill or jaded emperors, courtiers, and daimyo were continually trekking to the hot springs and famous sights. They have left an ample body of poems, travel stories, and diaries, which now are eagerly exploited for their publicity value. I have already mentioned, in this connection but with a more modern touch, Anchiku's "Weston Festival," which the National Railways advertises on station billboards across the country. A more humble example is afforded by the Ariake confectioner. One of his products is a fairly standard bean-jam bun (*monaka*) of a sort locally prepared throughout Japan. On the front of its wrapper appears a halftone of Mount Ariake circled with clouds, and the label *Shinano Fuji Monaka*. On the back is a poem by the Emperor Gotoba (1180–1239), who effuses about being wrapped in stiff-shouldered garments in a cold downpour and glimpsing the white clouds wrapped about Mount Ariake.

Long vacations are uncommon except among the upper classes or among farming families who rent cheap rooms at a hot spring during the agricultural slack season. The 1947 labor laws, as we have seen, require an annual paid vacation of at least one week for regular employees. But salarymen have a reputation for being reluctant to claim all their allotted days. In part this is a demonstration of loyalty, but in part it may be a desire for extra income, since some firms pay a premium for working during vacation.

Not all vacations are used for travel, of course, but it is a favorite activity. Recent surveys show that about one out of two urban heads of household, and one out of three adults in general, has a pleasure trip longer than overnight at least once a year. In all of the fifty Anchiku families that my assistants and I studied (twenty in Ariake, twenty in Eitai-machi, ten in Hikari-ga Oka) at least one member of the family had been able to take a vacation trip of two or three days during the preceding year. And at the upper limit there were young marrieds who were on the go nearly every month.

Whole-family vacations are said to be rapidly increasing, but they still are unusual by American standards. Except in the upper classes or among newlywed urbanites the family is likely to travel together only for visits to distant kin. One survey by the Prime Minister's Office in November, 1960, found that of those who had taken a vacation trip the previous year, only one-fourth had been accompanied by the rest of the family. A husband and wife—most often urban but occasionally rural—may get away once or twice a year for a night together at a resort; in the vernacular it is called going *abekku* (French *avec*).

But in general, vacation trips are made with peers. Since early Meiji, schoolchildren have been going on annual school study tours, some local but always one or two to Tokyo or to Kyoto-Osaka. (The National Railways has a full-time train on the east-west main line reserved exclusively for such tours.) Young adults travel with Youth Groups or organize their own parties for skiing, hiking, or *wandāfōgeru* (German *Wandervogel*). Husbands tend to travel with men from the shop, or with commercial or professional associates—cf. Mr. Akinai and his fellow grocers. Wives' tours are arranged by the Women's Clubs (group travel by women, except for grannies on pilgrimages, was rare before the war). And even the Old Folks' Clubs take an occasional outing, usually to one of the postwar resorts that calls itself a *herusu sentā* ("health center"). What J. A. R. Pimlott has said of his fellow Britons can be said as well of these English of the Far East, that vacations have become a modern cult. "For many they are one of the principal objects of life—saved and planned for during the rest of the year, and enjoyed in retrospect when they are over." Vacation detritus is visible in every Anchiku living room, in the form of souvenir paintings, *kokeshi* dolls, plastic models of Tokyo Tower, and albums of snapshots unwrapped to show to the inquisitive foreigner.

A Tradition Continuing

As with Walpole's Englishmen, the Japanese like ducks seem forever to be waddling to the waters. It is a poor vacation that does not include a stopover at a mineral hot springs resort (*onsen*). There are more than 1,300 onsen in the islands, in almost every conceivable setting, offering almost every conceivable form of entertainment. Those near the great cities have become stocked with chrome and concrete pleasure palaces in the postwar years, but those in a hinterland such as Anchiku preserve a rustic flavor. One feels that some sort of pinnacle is being attained in the "New World" center under construction on the beach at Atami, southwest of Tokyo. In addition to two hotels and several restaurants (one a drive-in), the "New World" will offer a roller coaster, observation tower, sightseeing ropeway, artificial waterfall, marina, showboat, suspension bridge, marineland, artificial caves and undersea tunnel, fishing ponds, tennis courts, swimming pools with seawater and mineral water, and space for further discoveries. By contrast, in Anchiku only the largest and most urban onsen, Asama in the northeast suburbs of Matsumoto, offers even a few pinball parlors and neon-festooned streets. Many Tokugawa daimyo maintained villas at onsen in their domains. And today, similarly, many government bureaus and large corporations provide inns or cottages free or at cut rates for employees and their families. Asama has a handful of such places, and Atami, according to one count, has more than 270.

Onsen-going is such conspicuous leisure that in constrictive periods it can easily stick in the moralist's eye; in the war years it was subject to public scrutiny. The government might openly appropriate onsen for use as rest-and-recreation centers—as in turn the Occupation did after 1945—or for domiciling schoolchildren evacuated from the cities. But ordinary citizens had to be circumspect with a war on. Notice the more-loyal-than-thou stance of the Preface to a 1942 Nagano onsen handbook:

Onsen have since ancient times played a major role in curing, in disease prevention, in bodily strengthening and even in spiritual cultivation. Therefore I think it no exaggeration to say that Japan is the world's greatest onsen nation and to underline the fact that onsen have constructed a powerful Japanese people. Riding the waves of changing times, not a few onsen were exploited as objects of commercial enterprise, suffered abnormal development at the hands of heartless people, and were degraded into objects of libertarian individual pleasure. The results influenced the very essence of the onsen, and it came about that users of onsen were even thought of as public enemies. In this regard people of heart criticized those who were speaking profanely of the miraculous springs, destroying the simple style and charming customs, and seeking to drive public morals to the depths; at the extremes some even attacked this as a transgression against the Japanese spirit. The basic efficacy of the onsen does not change; onsen became targets for critical attack as a result of thoughtless managerial methods on the part of some operators, and of users' unpatriotic attitudes. That now, in the Great Asian War, the onsen is being fundamentally re-examined by both sides, users and operators, and, smartly drawn back into its original form, is a phenomenon to bring joy to the nation.

In the 1960's, innkeepers no longer even furnish the police with a nightly guest list. The main value of the guest register now, say Anchiku owners, is as a mailing list for New Year's postcards. And onsen-going has regained imperial blessing. Just as the Kennedys have raised the fame of Cape Cod, so the Crown Prince has created a fashion for Karuizawa (over the hills east of Anchiku) by discovering his bride-to-be on the tennis courts there.

Otari Onsen

The name means "little valley." The valley, narrow and twisting, is in the hills twenty miles north of the Anchiku plain, close by the border of Niigata prefecture. The onsen, four inns pushed together in a seemingly planless tangle of roofs and balconies, perches a hundred feet above the valley floor in the upper reaches. It is off the main route from Anchiku to the Japan Sea; even the footloose Reverend Weston bypassed it. Today the bus from Ōmachi at the north end of the plain consumes two and a half hours getting there. Except for a few sections through some villages, none of the road is paved —a ribbon of ruts, holes, sharp turns and cliff-clinging. Where a washout remains unrepaired, the bus at times bumps along the dry bed of the Hime River. When it reaches Nakatsuchi it turns up into the little valley and begins a steep climb to the onsen at 2,400 feet.

Until 1955 Otari did not have the bus. From Nakatsuchi one either had to walk or hire a horse, although sometimes a jeep or rugged small truck could navigate the trail. "If anything, service is worse now," remarks Yamada Hiroshi, master of the Yamada-kan, largest and oldest of the Otari inns. "Snowslides and landslides are pretty common around here, and now it may take two or three days to get the road cleared. The horses could always walk around. Not that it's a serious problem. We just have to do without the papers for a few days."

The onsen was founded in the Kōji era (1555–1558), legendarily by survivors from the Takeda-Uesugi war on the plain. It has been in continuous use, first as a villa for the Matsumoto lords, and since the 1870's as a commercial enterprise. The villa became the nucleus of the Yamada-kan (later rebuilt and enlarged); the three smaller inns were erected by newcomers from Niigata in the Meiji period. Adventurous urbanites began coming in small numbers by the turn of the century, and Otari began to issue advertising leaflets. But until the end of the war more than four-fifths of the clients were villagers from Anchiku and Niigata. They came during the agricultural slack season, carrying their own rice and vegetables and beanpaste, renting rooms with kitchen privileges. They stayed two or three weeks, bathing, relaxing, visiting—for neighbors and fellow villagers often came in groups. Some hamlets have been sending regular delegations annually since the late nineteenth century. And although the custom has declined rapidly in postwar years, as farmers have become able to travel elsewhere inexpensively, it was maintained through the war.

"There seldom were many guests in the war years," says Mr. Yamada, "but at times we could almost pretend the war didn't exist. Up here we never once lacked for food. Old customers appeared at their usual times. We weren't called on to house refugees. When the news got bad we would shut off the radio for a few days."

The clientele has been growing more diverse since 1945 and especially since the bus road was opened. Otari now attempts to lure skiers in the winter (there were a few even before the war) and it advertises over Tokyo radio networks for students on wandāfōgeru in the summer. Additional rooms are built from time to time to meet the expanding demand, but the Otari operators have elected not to undertake a sweeping modernization. "We probably could attract an even wider clientele by modernizing," says Mr. Yamada, "but at the risk of sudden swings in trade. As it is, our trade is dependable and its fluctuations predictable. People rarely come this far without reservations, except for some of the old villagers. Most of the other mountain onsen have become citified already; it will be worth our while to maintain our family atmosphere. Most of our guests come here because of the quiet and the scenery and the mountain cuisine. A few years ago when pinball games were such a rage we installed a few machines. But there was no profit in it. Even men who play regularly at home found it was no fun playing here without their usual cronies around."

(Not far away, around Hakuba and Yotsuya, the arcadian touch has been carried a step further. The area has won a national reputation for "rustic rooming" in which urban skiers are put up in local farmhouses.)

Rates at Otari as elsewhere vary of course with service and facilities. The basic cost per person runs from 400 to 1,200 yen for a standard unit: room for a night, bath, dinner, and breakfast. (At Asama one would be charged about twice as much, at Atami thrice.) Groups who are willing to crowd together can obtain discounts. Wandāfōgeru, for example, pay about 350 yen a day, including a noon meal. Guests who cook their own meals pay 200 yen a day for room, dishes and utensils, firewood, and access to a kitchen.

In addition to the four inns, Otari has two shops selling souvenirs and sundries, and a taxi stand. A barber from down the valley can be called in during the summer months; a masseuse comes periodically from Niigata and stays a few days. The inns now have television receivers; before that *naniwa-bushi* singers wandered in occasionally, and Mr. Yamada sometimes rented movies. But the more notorious "water-trades" have never been welcomed. "Geisha can be called in from Ōmachi or Itoigawa," says Mr. Yamada, "but the expense is awesome, and only once or twice a year does a guest feel up to showing off that much. Most of the time they try to coax the maids into sitting with them and pouring for them. The maids aren't supposed to, but they are just country girls and can be prevailed upon."

The mineral waters, which gush out at 46° centigrade, are considered efficacious for a wide range of ailments, including gastrointestinal disorders, women's diseases, nervous diseases, skin afflictions, and rheumatism. Otari has a small but steady stream of guests seeking cures or relief. Some of them stay several weeks. Other guests stay about a week on the average, resting or exploring the nearby ski slopes and hiking trails. Now with the bus road open, there have begun to be a few groups of teachers, officials and salarymen on overnight binges, and more rarely a youth group or women's club. This sort of trade is still minor, though, in contrast to what it is at more accessible onsen such as Asama or Yamabe.

"Each kind of group has its drawbacks," one inn-keeper remarked to me. "The women are quiet and don't break things up, but they'll quibble with you about the number of slices of raw fish you serve. Politicians and bureaucrats are bossy but they spend openly. For some reason the schoolteachers really tend to cut loose, and so do some of the youth groups. I don't worry if the boys come in ordinary clothes, but if they come in their fire brigade coats there's sure to be trouble."

Mr. Yamada has evolved a rule of thumb for drinking

parties: if the men have more than three bottles of sake apiece, trouble is likely. "We try to persuade them not to drink any more, but of course they can always bring in sake from elsewhere. Or even worse, switch to whiskey. I scold them, warn them, if necessary drag them into separate rooms until they are quiet. We've never failed to quell a brawl, but I can't deny that they've been getting worse in recent years."

The Joiners

Ever since de Tocqueville called attention to it, Americans have thought of themselves as a nation of joiners. Associations are said to exist for every purpose. They also are said to foster democracy, and in good American fashion the Occupation leaders strived to sow PTAs, 4-H Clubs, and the like all over postwar Japanese social soil. Actually, joining does not seem peculiarly American in cross-cultural perspective. Associations seem to grow out rather regularly from human interaction everywhere, unless they are forcibly suppressed. And that has been their fate over much of the course of Japanese history. The environment has been more supportive since 1945, but until then even the most innocuous poetry club ran the risk of interdiction, above all during the militarist decade.

Americans tend to underline the voluntary aspects of association membership, Japanese are more aware of its compulsory facets—of the moral pressure of the waku. Either view by itself is incomplete. Not a few Americans find that they have "been volunteered" for participation in PTA's and charities; not a few Japanese find it exciting to take active roles in community associations even though all residents may be members by definition. But each view indicates the parochial climate of opinion, and there is no doubt that Japanese have tended to be much more accepting than Americans of government surveillance and control of organizations.

The Neighborhood Associations are one good example. These are compulsory groupings of ten to twenty contiguous households, rural or urban. They have had active and dormant epochs, but for more than 600 years have been used in varying capacities as unpaid and quasi-official administrative organs. The closest American parallel is the Air Raid Block Warden organization of late World War II. In the Tokugawa era the Neighborhood Associations were collectively responsible for paying taxes and they were admonished to carry out mutual spying—to report a neighbor who was accumulating weapons, practicing Christianity, or engaging in other dangerous activities. After 1868 they lost legal standing and direct ties to higher governmental levels but continued to be used for administrative convenience by the village and ward. Once more in the militarist years they were made official, to be in turn "abolished" as totalitarian by the Occupation. Today they live on unofficially in most parts of Japan, although they probably are stronger in Anchiku than in the great metropolitan centers. In Eitai, for instance, the Neighborhood Association prepares and serves the feast, runs errands, and foots the bill for a wedding or funeral of any member household. The binding force is custom, not law; perhaps there is a parallel in neighborhood "gentleman's agreements" in the U.S. One relies upon his neighbor's good faith. One can ask to have a lavish feast, but with the understanding that his neighbor may later request the same.

In Ariake, similar functions are performed not by

the Neighborhood Associations but by multiple-purpose associations known as *Kōshin-kō*. They are religious in name and pedigree, but their six meetings a year are, like Kaempfer's holidays in Nagasaki, sacred rather to mutual compliments and civilities. After a short prayer the group spends an evening eating, drinking, and socializing. The group also maintains a contingency fund and sometimes owns a set of festive chinaware and eating trays. It serves at weddings and funerals (also digs the grave, since Ariake has no professionals to do this), although the host household is expected to bear the brunt of the expenses. Members tend to be chosen from noncontiguous and nonkin households. The argument is that at weddings and funerals the neighbors and kin should be free to take part in the ceremonies and not be burdened with the serving.

American sociologists sometimes classify associations as instrumental or expressive. If we apply this to Japanese associations, we find only a few in which one aspect predominates. Mr. Torii's Saturday Club seems mostly expressive; the Neighborhood Associations seem mostly instrumental. The main task of a Neighborhood Association leader is to carry information between the member households and the hamlet or street chairman. The leader—often simply called a "connector"—collects funds for the Red Cross or Community Chest, and he distributes tax forms, city hall notices, public health circulars, or, in special instances, an ethnographer's questionnaire. There is no compensation for this, and the office is regarded as a mild nuisance. Rural Neighborhood Associations also are responsible for the upkeep of paths and footbridges in their territory. These associations hold an annual party but have few other obviously expressive activities.

However, many associations which are important instrumentally also perform important expressive functions. For example, the Fire Brigade has obvious duties, and in Ariake hamlets all males between about twenty-five and thirty-five years must participate. (Age limits are adjusted as necessary to maintain the brigade at full strength.) But at the same time—this is the "whiling" problem on a broader timescale—entry into the brigade is an important mark of maturity, and its parties are expected to be manly ones, as we heard from the lament of the innkeeper quoted earlier. Because of this overlapping of functions, I find it more helpful to class associations by their manner of recruitment. On this basis one sees in Anchiku two major clusters of them, plus a miscellany of others.

The first major cluster centers around residence. All households in a residential community, whether an urban street such as Eitai or a hamlet such as one of the ten in Ariake, are by definition members of the Community Association. Each household has one vote in its affairs and is expected to send a representative to its meetings. Since the meetings usually consist of one annual plenary session for electing officers and holding a party—routine affairs are conducted through the neighborhood "connectors"—the duty is not onerous. The Community Association does not have taxing powers, nor does it own property other than an assembly hall. (It may or may not have one; Eitai does not.) Community holdings of arable land were forbidden in the postwar land reforms, although some remain by subterfuge. The chairman also tends to be little more than a link between the neighborhood "connectors" and city bureaus, although hopefully he will be a man capable of lobbying effectively at city hall. (For the past decade

Eitai has elected as chairman a resident politician who sits on the city council.) This side of the Community Association is mostly instrumental, but it also supports an expressive program through its Peoples' Hall.

The Peoples' Hall is nominally autonomous and has its own chairman to supervise the program. But it is closely linked to the Community Association and its membership is coterminous. (Occasionally the Peoples' Hall may include more than one community, as is the case for Eitai.) At the same time it is affiliated with the town or city Peoples' Hall. The latter has a full-time professional staff, which distributes subsidies to the community units and tries to influence their programming. Programs vary widely with local interest and leadership ability. Typically there will be a baseball team, track and field teams that compete in the annual village or ward athletic meet, and clubs for women, youth, and old folks. Associations may be included for special purposes, such as the silkworm raisers' groups in some Ariake hamlets.

The clubs in turn are nominally autonomous, although affiliated with their counterparts on district, regional, prefectural, and national levels. Before the war these hierarchal chains were used for central government direction and the issuing of patriotic propaganda. Viewing this in a Kyushu village in 1935, John Embree remarked of the associations that "their only possible common ground is nationalism—and therein lies the key to their existence. As a means of increasing national unity, they form part of the national policy, and, if the government and the school should cease to encourage them, they would die a natural death." The Occupation tried to cleanse the stigma from the system by placing program planning in community hands and by making participation elective. On the whole this seems to have accorded with community desires. The clubs, like fraternal organizations in America, are likely to take some of their cues from national headquarters, but can ignore it if desired. Likewise the local leaders are volubly aware that they cannot compel participation but must coax it through clever programming—classes in sewing or penmanship, a coöperative for child-care during transplanting and harvest, Christmas parties, onsen tours, or calling upon the ethnographer to show color slides of life in the United States.

The community Shinto shrine also is a part of this cluster. The 1947 Constitution insists upon a separation of church and state. But although the shrines are no longer subsidized by the central government, they are maintained locally as foci for community self-objectification. Only the obstinate fringe will refuse to contribute to shrine upkeep—more a civic than religious obligation. But annual tutelary festivals are becoming difficult to stage. This is only partly a result of the lure of commercial entertainment, for the festival still is a day "sacred rather to mutual compliments and civilities." The main problem is a severe exodus of young adults to the big cities. Ariake hamlets have Shrine Youth Groups to stage the festival, and participation in them is compulsory. But there are many complaints that this places upon a few households a duty that should be shared by all. Eitai shares a tutelary with a half dozen other streets. By calling out women and children too, each street can muster enough hands to drag its festival cart around the neighborhood. But in order to liven the affair, men students from Shinshū University are hired for the day to carry banners and portable shrines.

The other major cluster of associations centers around occupation—the corporations, labor unions, producers' coöperatives, professional societies, and merchants' leagues, whose instrumental goals are patent. The corporations are especially likely to offer "human relations" programs of as wide or wider a scope than those offered through the Peoples' Halls: classes in flower arranging or ceremonial tea for young women, a company chorus, athletic teams, group tours, and cheap vacations at the company villa. Some brand-name corporations even sponsor professional baseball teams. The range is much narrower for other occupational groups, but even the humblest shopkeepers' league has its blossom-viewing outing and a tour or two every year.

In the city these occupational ties crosscut residence ties. But in hamlets, where most people are farmers, the two criteria overlap through the local producers' coöperative. (Nonfarming residents are permitted to join the coöp as nonvoting affiliate members, though few see reason to.) The postwar coöps are empowered not only to engage in commerce but also to undertake broad programs in health, education, and recreation. They have their own women's auxiliaries and youth leagues, and special clubs for pig-raisers, dairymen, and so on. The membership and the programs both overlap widely with those of the Peoples' Hall, and a sort of ecological struggle is underway between the two. One can't help but suspect that if the Peoples' Hall lost its subsidies the coöperative would quickly surge ahead.

In addition to these two clusters one finds a miscellany of other associations. Some develop among neighbors—rotating credit clubs commonly do. But many recruit regardless of occupation or residence: pen-pals, amateur radio fans, stamp collectors, or nudists. Religious and patriotic organizations also tend to form in this way. Most households are affiliated with a temple for burial purposes, but neighbors commonly are members of different temples. Anchiku people tend to be proud of their irreligious stance, and on the whole the revitalizing "new religions" of the modern century do poorly here in contrast to the Kyoto and Okayama regions. My household interviews turned up only one case in fifty families, that one an Eitai craftsman.

Daria Gurūpu

From the conditions I have outlined, the reader can perhaps better comprehend Japanese attitudes toward the involuntariness of many associations. However, in the open tenor of postwar times energies have been put into groups of a more self-willed sort. The clubs under Peoples' Hall auspices are officially elective, although they carry residual overtones of civic duty. But there is greater freedom for the whole rainbow of workers' choruses, skin-diving clubs, or doll-making circles such as the one to which Mrs. Torii belongs. Significantly, associations of this kind usually have part-Anglo names: the "X circle" (*sākuru*), or "club" (*kurabu*), or "group" (*gurūpu*). Also, these are usually the only associations that Japanese social scientists mention favorably in connection with the after hours.

A now-hackneyed saying has it that "since the war two things have got stronger, stockings and women"; and younger women have been especially active in creating associations for themselves. This applies particularly to young wives. Traditionally the young wife has been near the bottom of the social ladder, scarcely outranking pariahs and aliens. As the samurai or salaryman role has been one to emulate, so hers has been one to avoid. She ranks lowest in her household; and although the saying "should we get us a cow or a young wife?" overpaints her low esteem it does give a measure of it. Brought into her husband's household, she is expected to adapt to its ways under the constant tutelage of her mother-in-law. She must bear this until the mother-in-law retires and allows her to succeed as full-fledged mistress of the household. Conditions are more favorable if she and her husband found their own home, but even so her lot is likely to be a lonely one. Even in premodern times custom allowed the young wife periodic vacations at her parental home (regional traditions vary on the particulars). And today with women's social standing generally higher, and with brides becoming reluctant to marry farmers, even the elders are trying to help make the young wife's role a more enjoyable one.

The *Daria Gurūpu* ("Dahlia Group") is an association of young wives in one Ariake neighborhood. It was organized in January, 1957, at the suggestion of the older wives (mothers-in-law), who for years have had a social club of their own. Membership in Dahlia is elective, but all fifteen young wives in the neighborhood have joined. They meet regularly once a month, with extra sessions for special events, such as when they were rehearsing a skit for presentation at the annual meeting of the Ariake Association of Women's Clubs. The group meets by turns at members' houses, during afternoons in the slack and colder winter months, during evenings in the busier and warmer summer months. There is no permanent leader. The hostess of the preceding meeting serves as the day's chairwoman. She is charged with collecting monthly dues of thirty yen and with keeping minutes of the meeting. She is encouraged not only to write a factual report but also to add her own impressions and reflections. The resulting record is a fascinating account of young wives' hopes, joys, and struggles. Some of the minutes are businesslike, such as this one:

> Events: Agenda for holding third annual meeting of young wives and mothers-in-law. Decided on a dinner party, etc. Date: November 19th. Place: home of Mochizuki Fusae. Menu: chicken and egg on rice, soup, broiled fish, bean-curds, eggwhirls. Prepare at Mrs. Tanaka Fumie's home, or if inconvenient there at Mrs. Arai Junko's home. Because of autumn harvest, October meeting cancelled, and attendance tonight poor. But confirmed plans for the party with the older wives' club as entered on this year's plan of operations. What with much conversation we went on past eleven o'clock, when we adjourned.

But many of the writers allow their feelings to show, albeit in a rather positive-thinking way:

> (1) Meeting had been suggested for 1:00 P.M. on January 26th during winter but was rescheduled for that evening at the host family's request. Evening brought a terrific rain and wind, and unfortunately the younger young wives who have babies and such to take care of didn't show up.

> (2) In reviewing the Dahlia Group's year's activities we noted that we had thought up a name for our club. We talked about many other things but mostly there was too much gossip. With regard to our plans for the coming year I think we should set out two or three topics and try to develop them:
>   a. reading club—circulate and read love novels and light books;
>   b. practice sessions in cooking suitable for farm families;
>   c. keep farm home budgets.

(3) We meet once a month and everyone enjoys it since we are always around the house and especially as young wives don't have opportunities to get out. When everyone is diligent about talking, you get to feeling good. You think that you are the only one with hurt feelings, but when everyone talks you realize it's the same for all. Dahlia Club is a place of relaxation, a place of consolation, a place for reflections, isn't it?

In its short career the group already has developed several regular activities. Some of these are of an instrumental nature, such as an annual disinfecting of all toilets in the neighborhood, or lessons on budgeting, family planning, and use of contraceptives. But the program includes many meetings just for sociability; an annual outing; and an annual dinner party for the older wives. This last usually spurs the chairwoman to rhetoric:

On the afternoon of November 16th the Dahlia Group all assembled and made the necessary preparations for the arrival of the older wives' club. We had been planning this since summer, and although it was difficult to realize, it finally had arrived as hoped-for. Thanks to everyone's skill we enjoyed a grand feast. We face our elders every day, and yet what were our thoughts on this day? Wasn't it great? I am delighted that everyone worked with all her might. For a half day, omitting nothing, we expressed our thanks to the older wives for their continual efforts in our behalf. I think next year we must plan to do something of the same sort again. From now on everyone in the Dahlia Club will be dreaming of how in ten years when she's gotten older she too will be treated in this way. Ten years—it's almost here!

The day I attended, all fifteen women were present, as were four toddlers who snuggled in their mothers' laps or quietly toyed with crackers. The topic was the annual outing, and some members pressed for a trip to Nagano City (which is two hours' ride by train and bus). The chairwoman demurred. She cited the expense, the bother of meeting bus and train schedules, the burden of looking after the children. "Let's wait for a sunny day in April. We'll go on our bikes to Hotaka; easy to take the kids that way. A lot of us still haven't seen the new Old Folks' Home, the Rokuzan Museum, or the reclamation project. We'll picnic on the riverbank—that'll make it easy for washing out dirty diapers." She carried the day.

Daily Diversion

The daily round also has its contemporary traditions of after hours activity, but most of them are so personal and intimate that they are inherently difficult to discuss in short compass. The savor of family conversation after dinner, the fellowship of salarymen having a whiskey-on-the-rocks in a "stand bar" on their way home, evening dabbling in the garden—to comprehend these one has to know the people involved.

The most regular item on the daily agenda in Japan as in the United States is some form of contact with the media of mass communications; newspapers, radio, and television. (And though it rarely is counted in survey research, we probably should include the daily delivery of mail, or its anticipation.) We come to expect seeing the day's paper in the house just as much as we expect seeing the other pieces of furniture in their accustomed locations. One Matsumoto salaryman remarked that even though he reads two or three newspapers in odd moments at the office he still has a Shinshū regional paper delivered at home. He rarely even looks at it, but the apartment would be "lonely" without it. The Japanese social psychologist Minami Hiroshi is explicit about this ritual aspect of the media:

By most of the audience the broadcast programs are received daily at a set time and a set place; they are a form of habitual activity, therefore they take on the propriety aspect of habit. Basically, a propriety psychology is in operation here, resembling the way one gains assurance by offering prayers to the gods at set times. To listen to a particular program every evening before retiring, and to go to bed having gained mental stability, is to anticipate psychological effects similar to the comfort one gains from prayer. In this sense mass communications can be called a "faith" of modern man.

Two recent social surveys both point up the overwhelming daily importance of the media. The 1959 study by the Tokyo University Newspaper Research Institute, mentioned in Chapter 4, asked its metropolitan Tokyo interviewees how many minutes they had devoted to various kinds of after hours activity the previous day. Mass media contact was far and away on top, with an average of 109 minutes. The two next largest categories were "doing nothing" (*bui*) with an average of forty-three minutes, and "sociability" (*kōsai*) with forty. A different measure was taken in a 1960 Economic Planning Board survey of 6,100 married couples, one-third rural and two-thirds urban, who were asked to name their three chief after-hours activities on an ordinary day. Again media contact led the field, being named by 88 to 90 per cent of the respondents in three categories, although it dropped to 78 per cent for rural wives. Activities which scored more than 10 per cent in any of the four categories are as follows:

153

| | urban | | rural | |
activity	husbands	wives	husbands	wives
radio, TV, newspapers	89.1	90.0	88.1	78.2
reading books	35.5	29.7	23.5	15.9
napping, resting	28.3	17.9	44.1	23.6
shopping, visiting	6.6	32.3	11.3	40.7
conversation	33.6	45.0	52.7	58.2
miscellaneous	6.3	10.3	25.9	37.8

Several comments are in order. First, I have omitted from the table crafts, sports, gambling, movies, drinking, strolling, board games, and travel, all of which scored less than 10 per cent.

Second, the much higher percentage of miscellaneous replies from rural respondents very likely reflects a higher degree of "polychronicity" than that of more single-minded urbans.

Third, as the table indicates, a goodly number of wives do some shopping almost every day—even the ordinary Ariake housewife is likely to trot up to Schoolville fairly often for a piece of fish or some fresh cabbage, and the trip is also a convenient excuse to get out of the house and chat with other shoppers.

Fourth, the survey did not ask about diaries; but my Anchiku interviews revealed that a few men keep them, and nearly every housewife makes notes on recent happenings in the margins of her budgetary notebook. However, deep soul-baring is more for adolescent girls or for an adult with literary inclinations. (The diary is a favored literary form in Japan, and also is used in one brand of Japanese psychotherapy.)

Fifth, with regard to the high percentage of napping farmers, a similar tendency exists in the United States, and is similarly more prevalent among men than among their wives. Japanese commentators have been irked by what they consider unduly high percentages for napping. It seems so backward in a day when leisure should, they feel, be active. But the napping and "just resting" percentage does not seem too unreasonable—quite apart from the fact that some people *do* get worn out by heavy labor—when considered in the context of the daily round. Even with compulsive planning, one is likely to encounter brief "idle" intervals, after lunch, say, or before dinner. Aware that other activity is soon to begin, one may see little point to trying to accomplish anything. One might switch on a disk-jockey show, or thumb through the daily paper—both designed precisely for such casual moments. Or one might simply sit quietly. An outsider aware of the emphasis in Japanese poetry upon savoring the momentary might wonder if the ability to do so is more widespread in Japan than elsewhere. My impression is that it is not. Furthermore, only the most voracious reader or avid hobbyist is likely to continue his activity day after day. This may explain a seemingly low score for gambling, drinking, strolling, and the like. One turns to these of an evening when there is no other special event—a club meeting, a visitor, a shrine festival, or a more unusual happening such as a political rally. But one does not engage in them every evening.

Of an Evening

A political rally is not a "typical" daily event except for politicians, but perhaps by describing one I can give some sense of how a pleasant July evening might be passed in Ariake.

There had been handwritten posters on the neighborhood bulletin boards since the beginning of the month.

Printed tissues bearing the same message were inserted in the morning newspapers. The Preparatory Organizing Committee for the Nomura Association (they said) Presents an Evening of Lectures and Movies. Three lectures, plus a dramatic film. Nomura, an Anchiku man now a Representative in the Diet, will tell of his trip through Europe and Southeast Asia. Someone from the House of Councillors is to speak of recent Diet happenings—for in July, 1960, village conversation still is taken up by the Hagerty incident, the Zengakuren demonstrations, the death of Miss Kamba. And a third speaker, an obscure prefectural assemblyman—and only here does the purport begin to show—will discuss Social Democrat farm-village policies and programs.

The meeting is held in a hamlet Peoples' Hall near the center of the district. The lecture titles from the handbills appear again in bold brush strokes on three white paper banners that hang from the arch to the footlights of the little stage, blocking the view to the sheet hung as a movie screen. In front of the stage is a small table with a pitcher of water and a pot of flowers. To the left are three straight-backed chairs, their plush seats sloped and lumpy with age. Behind them is a blackboard on a tripod, and chalked on it in a clerical hand a detailed agenda of Calls to Order, Greetings, Introductions, Three Banzais for Nomura, and so on.

By 8:25—the handbills said eight sharp—enough people have collected to make it worthwhile to begin. They sit on the floor, chattering and lighting cigarettes. At the door a man distributes packets of reading matter. Each has three issues of *The Socialist Weekly*, with page-one editorials by Nomura. Also included are two leaflets, one that describes the party's aims and one that invites new members, with special notes addressed to farmers, fishermen, housewives, young people, and workers in small enterprises. And there is a cluster of mimeographed sheets of graphs and tables—prefectural variations in the spread of television, regional differences in the standard of living, international comparisons of caloric intake versus per capita income, and so on.

About twenty men and a half dozen women are present. Others straggle in from time to time. Nearly everyone has brought a small cushion; those who forgot, fold their jackets and sit upon them. The speakers stride from backstage and are ushered to the chairs; these they decline in order to sit on a level with the audience. An older man in the front row stands to say that he has been asked to serve as interim chairman. With his back to us, and with dramatic nods, he studies the agenda, turns, and calls order. Again he studies the agenda, then asks the party faithful to step to the back room to elect permanent officers. As a half-dozen men stand to leave, he suggests that Nomura use these minutes to introduce himself.

He has straight limbs, youthful face, sober brown suit. In his mid-forties, although I tend to underestimate Japanese ages. The soft-speaking manner and downturned eyes of a schoolteacher. He leans to one side as if groping for support there in the open in front of the table. He was a man who had given little thought to a political career, he tells us; just an ordinary salaryman in the electric works at T————— up the valley. One day the union sent word that somebody from the shop should run for the prefectural assembly, and for some reason he was put up. He won, and thanks to everyone's help has been winning since. He was sent up to the Center (i.e., Tokyo) and from there recently was included on a team studying parliamentary procedures in Europe and Asia.

Through it all he has always hewed to one principle—one that the present administration lacks—and this is, sympathy for the other fellow. After all, did Prime Minister Kishi really show any consideration for President Eisenhower and the situation he had been put in? Here's what I mean by sympathy, Nomura continues, a few years ago when I was still an assemblyman my little boy and I were walking downtown in Matsumoto. As we passed a toy shop all of a sudden the boy had a wild craving for a tricycle. Now there was no reason in the world why an assemblyman shouldn't have 1,300 yen in his pocket (I still remember the price). Like any father I wanted my boy to have a tricycle. But then I thought of all the boys in the neighborhood whose fathers would not have 1,300 yen in their pockets (things were rougher then, you know). And I had to stand and tell my boy he could not have it.

After five minutes, Nomura sits. The electors rename the old man as permanent chairman, and he launches into a formal introduction for Nomura, an oratorical display that scarcely seems extemporaneous. There are stirrings as the crowd settles into speech-hearing postures. About sixty are present now. A few are against the back wall, drowsing, ostentatiously awaiting the movies. But most faces are attentive, willingly suspending disbelief.

Again Nomura's quiet didactic tones. We all agree on what we want Japan to be, he says, a place where daily life is comfortable, peaceful, secure. But the mistake that some people make is in assuming that this can be done at a stroke, when what is needed most of all is moderation. This is our party's policy, and it is the policy that has been so successful for European socialism. We must proceed step-by-step (using the Anglo phrase), avoiding

158

both the upheavals of class-struggle revolution on the Left and of self-seeking militarism on the Right.

He goes on to describe glowingly what he had seen and experienced in England and Germany. These are things we can do in Japan, he says, and we can start right now. One of the first things we must do is to stop stuffing ourselves with rice. You'll see what I'm driving at if you will look at the data sheets that were handed out. As the cultural level of a nation rises, the consumption of rice goes up—to a point—and then it falls off, to be replaced by fruit, wheat, meat, and milk. This came home to me on my tour. In India, in Southeast Asia, in Egypt, they eat large amounts of rice but not so much as we do. In Europe on the other hand they eat almost none. We Japanese right now are at the peak of that curve, stuffing our bellies with three and four bowls of rice a meal even though we know good and well it's bad for us. It is time for us to start the downturn.

Now of course you realize what that will mean for you in the villages. It means learning to grow more wheat, learning to operate communal dairy herds. Not overnight. Don't rush right out and buy cattle. Let's do it step-by-step, with full consideration for local conditions and with continual support from the Center. We won't force theoretical schemes as in Russia and China. Let's make ours a genuine socialism. It also means that factories must be brought into the countryside. Right now I am working on a bill that will require that industry be dispersed across the nation—*require* it. Then those younger sons and daughters that you don't need in the fields will be able to find good jobs, and they won't have to go to Tokyo or Osaka to do it.

He talks about half an hour, his voice rising, warming, yet never losing its tone of friendly instruction. He closes by wishing to thank everyone personally, but alas he must speak at yet another meeting tonight. There is heavy applause, but Nomura is out the door before the chairman can organize the agenda's Three Banzais. A motorcycle explodes into action at the door and fades off along the main road.

Meanwhile the Assemblyman has been swiftly introduced and is speaking dutifully and dully, as though he were reading a financial statement. He seems never to get around to farm-village policy, his mind being taken by an ongoing struggle to amalgamate Nagano Prefecture with Shizuoka. The audience is lost to him. They turn to conversing, smoking, leafing through the handouts. Polite clapping punctuates his conclusion.

The Councillor follows, a leonine man of handsome white hair and eyebrows, of the smooth phrasing and practiced gestures of the lifelong politician. Again the plea for moderation, this time in regard to avoiding the international shame of demonstrations. A friend of mine just returned from America, he says, and I asked what the Americans are thinking. They don't know what to think, my friend told me. And do you blame them? Why should Eisenhower be turned away at the front door because of an unruly few when Khrushchev, the enemy himself, can go to America and get a warm welcome . . .

But the hour is late. In the back the movie awaiters are awake and restless. After fifteen minutes a note is carried up to the Councillor. Interrupted scoring a point, he is confused. But I have so much more to say, he pleads, glaring at the note. He resumes his lectern voice for a few sentences, finds his point, strikes it, then in the same breath asks peevishly, "What do you mean by just five minutes more?"

"If you don't leave then you'll miss the last train into

town," says the chairman mildly. There is a ruffle of snickers. But the words continue to bubble out well beyond the deadline. Two of the faithful discuss in loud whispers which of them will forego the movie to scout up a three-wheel truck and drive the Councillor back to town. At last the man is done, and he shuffles out with eyes burning.

One of the faithful rushes forward and tears down the paper banners, baring the screen. About twenty women and children hurry in from the entryway and find seats. A few men take up their cushions and leave. A buzzer growls, and the room collapses into darkness. The films are jumpy with age, sickly brown in tone from waterstains on the screen. First a newsreel, about two months out of date, showing May Day celebrations in Paris and Moscow, spring fashions, and the inevitable scenes of cleanup after the Ise Bay typhoon.

The feature is—of course—a swashbuckler. Its chief novelty seems to be that this time the invincible swordsman doesn't even need a sword. He duels with only a stout stick. After a few minutes I find it tedious, and a neighbor agrees. We feel our way to the door across the sprawling viewers.

Cooler outside, with a sliver of moon lending outline to the paths and paddies. The night air carries up the protests of the Nakabusa River as it scrapes against the stone levees thrown up after last year's flood. There is also the sound of our bicycle tires on gravel, and the rhythmic swing-swing of the headlamps before us. "I can't make up my mind," says the neighbor. "Should I sit up and read or should I try to get in a quick sleep? I have to be up by 4:00 A.M. to check the water levels in my fields."

アパート

7. *The Brighter Life*

Frequently there are criticisms of the tendency to pursue only pleasure in spare time. Isn't it more problematic to try to pursue pleasure in spare time only?   FURUTA AKIRA

The After-Hours Man

The search for enjoyment is not limited to the after hours, and to understand it we must see beyond clocks, clubs, and vacations. We must also see after-hours man and his way of living. Transformations in scheduling epitomize the modern condition, yet are only a part of it. In Japan, as in the West, the goal is not merely to increase the after hours and energize their uses. Agrarian despotisms have done as much. The goal is a new vision of man's place in a world of industrial democracies. It is a world whose received values do not always confer honor upon the situations in which men and women find themselves. It is a world in need of redefinition.

No such single and startling redefinition has taken place in twentieth-century Japan, although change has followed upon change in every corner of society. But the rudiments of redefinition appear in all varieties of Japanese visionary thinking, from political utopias to the arcadias of popular remembering, from religious green pastures to the blue skies of mass advertising. Politically, for instance, one thinks of the "four pillars" scheme of Eda Saburō, Secretary General of the Socialist Party. "The Soviet and Chinese Socialist construction formulas may look attractive to the world's backward nations, whose social structures resemble those of pre-revolution Russia and China," says Eda, "but not to Japan, where productivity is high, the social structure has been modernized and democracy exists, if not in perfect form." Accordingly, he argues, a new program for Japanese socialism must be built upon the "four pillars" of modern achievement: American material progress, Soviet social security, British parliamentary democracy, and Japan's own antiwar constitution.

In religious areas, again, one finds many examples in the revitalizing movements and revivalist cults. Japanese religions have long had a cheerful aura about them, but it seems prominent in these modern sects. Tenri, one of the largest and most firmly established of them (2.5 million members), has "happy living" (*yokigurashi*) as a central tenet; and the theme is lived out quite concretely by some of the smaller groups. For instance the Perfect Liberty League (*PL Kyōdan*, it uses the roman initials in its name) regards itself as a "religion of art" and seeks to make an art of the processes of daily living. Perfect Liberty maintains its headquarters on a golf course near Osaka and is noted for being sports-minded. Other sects exhibit a more highbrow inclination, and some have erected artistically furnished mundane "paradises" as models of the beautiful life. That of *Sekai Kyūsei* ("World Messianity") for example being on a hillside overlooking the same Atami where one finds the commercial "New World."

From these phenomena does not emerge a profile of after-hours man as sharp and as unequivocal as that of Ninomiya. But on the projective screens of Japanese desire we can at least glimpse his contours—albeit nebulous contours, since rigorous methods of "content analysis" are useless on so wide a scope. Physically he is at home in the material plenty of industrial production; mentally he strives to expand the experiential world of the self; socially he acts within a framework of peers, wife, and children. We would not be too wide of the mark if we imagined him as a salaryman, casually dressed, eight-millimeter camera in hand, strolling with his family on a sunny Sunday afternoon. In the darling phrase of the advertisers, his is the "brighter life" (*akarui seikatsu*). It is brighter in a very literal way, with its turquoise tractors, gay-tiled kitchens, or gaudy jackets. ("You sure could tell who the old man was," grumbled a fiftyish Ariake neighbor after visiting a ski resort. "I was the only one there with a black overcoat.") It is brighter too in its expectation of continuing prosperity and opportunity. (Where ten years ago underemployment was feared, now "help wanted" signs are seen all over Matsumoto.) And it is brighter for its faith in the possibility of social peace and personal fulfillment.

More whimsical—but also more revealing since it includes after-hours woman—is the public dream-work of Takechi Tetsuji in his tour-de-force on "Women's Life Ten Years From Now." Takechi depicts the daily round of a wife in 1970 in a typical middle-class family with a salaryman husband and two primary-school-age children. They live in a Tokyo suburban apartment with four rooms: bedroom, children's room, kitchen, and parlor.·

The 1970 wife arises at 9:00 A.M., and prepares breakfast in less than five minutes. (In 1956, according to a national survey by the Japan Broadcasting Corporation, 58 per cent of Japanese women were up by 6:30 and 98 per cent by 8:30 on ordinary days.) She merely heats the pancakes she prepared the night before while watching television, opens a bottle of "chlorella milk," and sets out cheese and jam (for calories). The children breeze in, trailed by their father with his typical male morning-face. "The sour face is still the same as ten years ago, as some of the habits of those days remain. Today's young men would certainly never make this kind of face in front of a woman."

The husband dials the phone, and the morning sono-news sounds through the room. Writing is almost unseen now, except for roman letters used for labels and signs, or symbols for mathematical and scientific formulae. Electronic progress has changed the age of print into an age of sound. Children no longer are crushed under the burden of having to learn 2,000 Chinese characters, the Japanese syllabaries, and the roman alphabet. Reading, penmanship, and composition have been replaced by simple lessons in speaking and listening; the school workday has been cut and does not begin until 10:00 A.M. Furthermore, the new technology makes it possible to alter the speed of a sound tape without altering its pitch, so that one can listen at the speed most comfortable to his ear. This husband, for example, prefers to hear the sono-news at 1,000 syllables a minute. But his children can readily take 2,000 syllables at school, and specialist scholars are able to absorb up to 5,000.

After the children leave, the husband sits sipping coffee. He does not leave for the office until noon, since he currently is on the afternoon shift from 1:00 to 7:00 P.M. He still commutes by bus. The family has a car, but Japan's roads are as bad as ever, so they use it only for shopping and pleasure trips.

Now comes the wife's afternoon ennui. These days a wife has very little washing or cleaning or even food preparation to occupy her. In the old days a wife was admired as a homemaker, but now she isn't much needed around the house—it is a form of hidden unemployment. Her younger sister stops by to visit. Though she is but six years younger, one can see in her how the tide has turned. The younger sister is a "business girl" who works the morning shift, and she hasn't the faintest desire to relinquish her career for boring housework. "She regards her elder sister who ten years earlier hastily gambled her life in marriage as having a curious existence."

With so much free time, recreation takes on massive significance. Today is the day of the Oakes, one of the five classic horseraces of the year. Baseball already is out of fashion. Baseball games take two hours or so to play, and that is much too slow for the modern mind; a race is over in minutes. The bookies come around to every house—as in the American system. And most wives have gambled themselves into debt to their bookie—another evil American influence. After the sisters place their bets, the wife sets out an early supper for the children. She tucks them away in their room, and the sisters depart to pick up the husband at seven and be at the racetrack by eight. There they ride the escalator up to the air-conditioned grandstand with its great view-windows, where the younger sister's date awaits her. The two couples, their emotions wrung by the races, have tea afterward and drive home quietly. The younger sister and her date ask to be dropped at a night club, since the hour still is early, only 1:00 A.M. (The 1956 survey found 67 per cent of all Japanese in bed by 10:30, 98 per cent by 12:30.)

As they near the American Embassy they discover, just as ten years ago, a student demonstration against the renewal of the Security Treaty. This time the Treaty surely will fail to be extended; there have come to be too many ugly memories. The main islands were spared, but Okinawa has become a death island of eternal silence ever since the bomb fell on it. "Cutting preferential national ties may invite temporary suffering. But then at last the true joys of peace and independence will be revived. In them alone is born the genuine pleasure of human living. If they are lacking, real happiness and the joys of a woman's life cannot possibly be brought into being."

Through his conceits Takechi discloses a serious commentary, and this is a point to be kept in mind. Although after-hours man is sometimes burlesqued, most often he cuts a serious figure. Writing of the American situation, Sebastian de Grazia has said, "The genius of the present industrial world is that it has given everybody, even the most unsuccessful of the lowest workers —the sense of having almost reached the land of Cockaigne. Ease and abundance are always nearly at hand. People shall have everything they want, and leisure too. Actually the singers of Cockaigne take themselves less seriously. They play on a world where you live without working, where you see with your stomach's eyes, and they know it's a dream, perhaps a lie. Sometimes they use the satiric style, or else a comic tone that shows they are laughing at themselves." Many schemes and dreams manifest current Japanese hopes, aspirations, or reaction-formations against only half-sensed frustrations. Their meaning is *not* always certain, for like all forms of metaphor they are, to borrow Suzanne Langer's dictum, ways of coping with a situation in which apprehension outruns comprehension.

A People of Plenty

By W. W. Rostow's calculations Japan was on the eve of an age of "high mass-consumption" in 1940. War and its aftermath delayed the dawn for more than a decade; but from the mid-1950's onward prosperity began to startle the Japanese themselves almost as much as the rest of the world. Gross national product has been increasing by nearly nine per cent a year, and Japan now ranks fourth among major industrial powers, trailing only the United States, the Soviet Union, and West

Germany. Signs of plenty are everywhere. By the 1960's, for instance, the Japanese began drinking more beer than sake; the Postal Ministry was offering transistor radios and foam-rubber mattresses in its New Year's lottery; the Emperor and Empress were reported to be living in "snug comfort" in their new residence; and "Dreamland," a Japanese version of Disneyland, opened its gates near the ancient capital and high-culture center of Nara. "TV is spreading, and sumo and baseball are becoming conversation topics for nearly everyone," writes essayist Ōno Tsutomu. "Weekly magazines are inundating us; the number of Torys Bars expands; in the coffeehouses, neatly dressed people listen to mood music; in the newspapers, electric appliances and department stores and movies are advertised brazenly; crowds are packed in at auto shows; girls parade at fashion shows; the ski slopes and swimming beaches are filled to capacity; the onsen centers are in a construction rush . . . and so on. If one tries to offer examples, there is no stopping point."

Viewing these developments through American lenses, Frank Gibney has termed Japan "The New Far West." And if one agrees with David Potter's thesis that *abundance* and not simply open land has been the great American frontier, Gibney's label is even more apt. As Potter phrases it, it was "abundance in any form, including the frontier form, rather than the frontier in any unique sense, which wrought some of the major results in the American experience. The frontier remained of primary significance precisely as long as it remained the lowest threshold of access to America's abundance . . . abundance, by contrast, has remained of primary significance both in the frontier phase and in the vast industrial phase which has dominated American life for the past three-quarters of a century."

The ordinary Japanese adult, schooled to believe that his land is poor and overpopulated, tends to balk at such terms. Measuring himself against American levels of consumption—as depicted in Hollywood movies or modeled on the spot by free-spending GIs and tourists—he is awed by the gap that remains. Told they are among the world's affluent peoples, my Anchiku neighbors consistently replied with bemused silence or embarrassed smiles. Of course the times are good, they would say. And, of course, the masses in Africa and South Asia still face starvation. But with the memory of wartime scarcity still in the stomach how does one respond to relative plenty? The old agrarian and nationalist slogans are threadbare. Nevertheless, even if per capita income is doubled by 1970 it still will be but a fourth or fifth of that in America.

The situation is in a way unprecedented. One fumbles even to find a label for it. Alien words are sampled—leisure, *vacance*, enjoy—and the repository of traditional images is scanned. After all, Japan had known prosperity in the past; she embarked upon modernization with what probably was the highest standard of living in Asia in the 1860's. Kaempfer in the seventeenth century marveled at the mounds of merchandise in Genroku shops and reported that in Kyoto "there is nothing that can be thought of, but what may be found." Allusions to Genroku luxury can be found even today in that cult of plenty, advertising. Yet it does seem that in none of the earlier periods were the material goods of life so widely shared as they are today. Today's prosperity is a democratic one—the term is justifiable even though vast income differentials continue.

In this sense there *is* a millennial atmosphere. And in fact the popular press has been fond of reviving symbols from the golden age of Japanese prehistory. The booms of recent years bear labels from the arcadias of the long-ago. The "Jimmu Boom" of the 1950's ties the name of the first emperor to the Anglo word "boom" (*būmu*) as if to say that it is the greatest period of prosperity since the founding of the empire. The "Iwato Prosperity" (*Iwato keiki*) alludes to an episode from the early mythology. In this episode—familiar to all Japanese schoolchildren—the Sun Goddess had grown peeved because her people had misbehaved (the war?) and had shut herself into a rock cave. To lure her out again the other gods on the high reed plain of heaven staged a roaring party. There was drinking and wild dancing and laughter, a sort of primordial *dolce vita*. Even the Sun Goddess could not resist this. She peeped out, the rock door (*iwato*) was rolled away, and brightness returned to the world.

Many writers also have punned upon the three imperial treasures. Historically these are the sword, mirror, and jewel of the imperial regalia. Now as the "three imperial treasures of the cultured life" they are counted in triads of consumer durables—for example, a car, a room cooler, a refrigerator. There are strong factors of facetiousness in this, to be sure, though perhaps no more than should be expected in the milieu. But the contrast with the sober, pompous use of the same symbols a wartime generation ago could not be more marked.

A less humorous development has been taking place at the larger and more famous Shinto shrines. Divested of government support by the Occupation, they have had to seek new sources of income. Many have turned to performing weddings, encouraging tourists, renting space for meetings, or leasing portions of shrine land. (The latter has its humorous overtones since some of the leased land has been used for racetracks and amusement facilities. This has given rise to jokes about the husband who announces to his wife that he feels a call to pay his respects to the gods at Y————, where the racing season happens to be on.) The Hotaka shrine in Anchiku has been in existence for more than a thousand years. Its major deity, *Hotaka mi no kami*, once was celebrated as a god of war. This has not been a popular cause since 1945; instead, shrine officials have publicly related his virtues as a god of traffic safety. Annual ceremonies are held to bless vehicles, and in nearly every Anchiku taxi and bus a Hotaka talisman is mounted over the center of the windshield. The shrine is said to derive more than a million yen a year from this service. And in 1959 when a typhoon felled several great cryptomerias in one corner of the shrine compound, the section was cleared and leased to a driver-training school.

It is easy to join Veblen in sneering at the pecuniary emulations of the newly rich. Japan has had its quota of them, from the globe-trotting *narikin* of the early twentieth century to the conspicuous splendors of the shogunal mausolea of Nikkō to the still-remembered consumption heroes of Genroku. Best known were the Edo timber merchants Kinokuniya and Naraya, who, like potlatching Kwakiutls, fought with property. Kinokuniya, for example, sometimes hired songwriters to immortalize his conquests—and incidentally his enterprises; he discovered the singing commercial long before Madison Avenue. In one episode, when Naraya was relishing a snowy vista, Kinokuniya flung coins and cackled as a mob trampled the snow scuffling for them. In another—the lore is genuine, even if the events are not—he and Naraya were together at a teahouse. Kinokuniya ordered an enormous *manjū* (another form of bean-jam bun—

172

with sexual connotations) brought to his rival. The manjū was so huge it could not be got up the stairway, so Kinokuniya at once sent for carpenters to widen the staircase. When the cake was opened it proved to contain several hundred smaller manjū. Later Kinokuniya revealed that he had had a great pot cast especially for the occasion.

However, these consumption heroes seem even more distant from the Anchiku of today than Ninomiya in his heroic diligence. Furthermore, their modern counterparts—the starlet photo-interviewed in her airconditioned apartment, the sumo champion racing his Toyopet across the cover of a news weekly—seem more tame, although that may make them more easy to emulate. At any rate, most people find their income rising only slightly, if steadily. It suffices to allow planning a longer trip, installing a tile bath, sending the children for piano lessons or setting money aside for supporting them through college. (Personal savings continue at one of the highest rates in the world.) In short, the hunger for comfort and fun is real, but hunting for "kicks" is not common. The politicians frolicking in the Matsumoto castle readily drew scorn, and in Ariake one hamlet was gossiped about after it hired two Hotaka geisha to serve at its harvest celebration.

My Anchiku interviews included several families of means, but only one case of lavishness. In it, significantly enough, both husband and wife are employed in full-time salaried positions; they hire a neighboring wife to care for their son after school. Their living room, though mat-floored, is covered by a multicolored rug. It is furnished with three armchairs, a kneehole desk with swivel chair, a large stereophonic console, a wall of bookcases filled with new editions of collected works, two violins, a globe, curtains *and* drapes across the windows, and a framed print of *The Last Supper* (they are not Christians). All in a nine-by-twelve room.

Furthermore there is confidence that life will continue to grow materially better. Western stereotypes of oriental timelessness have derived from superficial awareness of a few philosophical notions, not from daily life. And given the great catalog of postwar improvements, if nothing more, the confidence seems reasonable: witness only the remarkable developments in home appliances, the elimination of tuberculosis and poliomyelitis as major diseases, or the technological revolution in agriculture. (When blight threatened portions of the rice crop in Ariake and Hotaka in 1960, helicopters were sent from Tokyo to dust it.) The Ōmoto sect has "progressiveness" as one of its Four Guiding Principles. The Sōka Gakkai promises that its followers will gain wage increases automatically, without having to resort to strikes. Sekai Kyūsei and PL Kyōdan, among others, proclaim it Japan's destiny to show the world an industrial model of beautiful living. And the advertisers of course never tire of singing the praises of technology. Their rhetoric of progress appears in almost every newspaper, and it appears as well in more humble forms. Here is part of a leaflet distributed in Ariake in 1960 as Schoolville was about to unveil its first service station:

Greetings on Our Opening

Good wishes during the height of the hot season

That barometer of the new age, the use of petroleum products, daily follows an upward path; truly it feels good to witness progress in production and consumption.

Now in response to your demands the only service station in the village with complete facilities has been started here.

From automobiles, autobikes, and motorbikes to agricultural engines, all fuels and lubricants, oil for your household oil stove, we handle all petroleum products. Our creed is service first! We await your patronage.

In these same months, in Ariake as in many parts of Anchiku, people were rummaging in their attics for dusty seed-oil lamps, threshing racks, and the like. These they contributed to the local schools, which were organizing permanent exhibits to testify to the children the realities of consumer betterment.

The Underdeveloped Self

Western thinking associates leisure with privacy and individualism. At the extreme, we sometimes are told that even games and group activities run counter to the "spirit" of leisure, which is supposed to be linked through its Greek etymons with the education and exploration of the self. The Japanese are beginning to speak in similar phrases—learnéd ones allude to the Greek concepts—when portraying an after-hours ideal who is readily responsive to his personal human potential.

Although Japanese writers often borrow Anglo words, such as individualism or privacy, I believe that these convey more force and assertiveness than is present in the general Japanese outlook. As to privacy, for example, none of the fifty Anchiku families acknowledges a "personal" space in its home, apart from children's study desks. And though many of them wish for more rooms, the wish is for space for the entire family. In none of them does a member sleep alone, and the very desire to do so would raise suspicions of deviancy. (The children of 1970 who are simply hustled off into their room are, after all, fictional.) Similarly with individualism, if we mean it in the seventeenth century sense of a philosophical premise that personal rights are paramount: this still appears to the ordinary Japanese to border upon nihilism.

What is at issue, rather, is a sense of what R. P. Dore has called "individuation," and what many scholars from Marx to C. Wright Mills have scorned as "alienation." The Western reader is thoroughly at home with the problem and its roots in the forced specialization and felt fragmentation of industrial society. He also knows the "search for identity" and the fear that we have lost the "inner-directed" courage which Riesman ascribes to our arcadian grandfathers. Japanese opinion leaders hold similar fears, and they quote Riesman and Mills and Marx, or in native terms urge their fellowmen to develop "actorness" (*shutaisei*) and "self-direction" (*jishusei*). Restated according to the paradigm of Chapter 4, the point is that group goals continue to be paramount, but now a powerful stress is placed upon premise four. So long as group goals are not in danger, members' personal needs must be supported. And today on the projective horizons there have begun to be thrusts against that "amazing and immoral doctrine" that state and family should not be judged in terms of happiness. One current Liberal-Democrat slogan, for example, promises "Advancing Japan—Enjoyable Life."

Although the problem is grounded in the structure of modern society, the Japanese may feel it in a distinctive way because of their experiences over the past generation. Having encountered rapid discontinuities in government, national purpose, social codes, and economic fortunes, perhaps the Japanese have been made more aware of the continuities of the self. (The premodern Japanese world view lauded the transitory quality of living—sought to grasp the essence of the haiku moment—

but tended to leave it at that.) Anyway, one can appreciate the puzzlement felt by people who vividly recall being pressed into ant-hill service to the state, when even the after hours had to be used for the sake of victory, and who now are told to be full of "self-direction." Furuta Akira writes:

What sort of thing is this "self as an individual"? The postwar Japanese became conscious during the war and the difficult conditions just afterward that it is above all "naked natural man," in short the instinctive, sensitive, complicated "actor of desires." At the same time, as one writer related, "The world changed. But whether under the Emperor system or within a democratic society, my instincts and passions did not change." The sentence shows well the discovery of the self as an unchanging "actor of desires" within a changing society.

This growing awareness of being an underdeveloped self in an overdeveloped social order is revealed in another way in polls taken of "dreams of youth." The table on page 178, adapted from data assembled by Takahashi Akira, offers a consistent direct trend from a high idealism in 1940 to a burgeoning escapism (Takahashi's labels) in 1959. It adds support to what one would expect from the age differentials in attitudes to work and leisure given in the table in Chapter 4.

Takahashi offers these figures as evidence for a growing political apathy among youth, whom he accuses of lacking both common sense and long-run objectives. (He seems to regard student demonstrations as of no meaning.) Like many Japanese intellectuals, left as well as right, he is ready to attack any signs of self-strengthening as signs of selfishness. Advocates of "self-direction" thus must choose their words carefully, lest urgings of inner-

177

		year (in percent)				
Attitude to Society	1930	1940	1950 (male)	1950 (fem)	1953	1960
REALISTIC	27.4	13.7	10.3	10.2	21	20
work hard and become rich	18.6	8.7	6.0	6.2	15	17
study hard and become famous	8.8	5.0	4.3	4.0	3	6
IDEALISTIC	56.8	76.3	40.9	40.3	39	29
reject injustice in the world and live in honesty and justice	32.6	40.4	28.9	32.3	29	23
devote oneself to society	24.2	35.9	12.0	8.1	10	6
ESCAPIST	15.7	7.1	45.7	46.5	32	45
pursue life congenial to one's tastes, regardless of money or fame	12.2	5.9	31.1	33.5	21	27
live a free-and-easy life	3.5	1.2	14.6	13.0	11	18
UNKNOWN	—	2.4	3.1	2.1	4	3

direction be misread as urgings of outer licentiousness. After all, they too are worried lest the after hours be "wasted" in the newborn but puerile rituals of mass distraction. The usual result is a redoubled insistence upon active personal selection, a sort of continual environmental testing rather than a passive accepting of what is offered by the mass media or the repertory of classical arts. Napping, or even casual television viewing—"napping in disguise"—come not to be looked upon as vestiges of old-fashioned fatalism.

Surely self-development can be a muscular ideal. It demands thought, planning, determination. It need not imply a negation of family, firm, and social framework: they continue to structure the environment of behavioral possibilities. "I affirm the pursuit of 'happiness,'" writes Furuta. "But it is not just an enjoyment of sensuous 'pleasures'; I believe it must include the 'joys' and 'delights' of struggling against complex, given, realistic conditions and thereby spontaneously realizing 'human possibilities.'" If the growing specialization of society has taken art, enjoyment, creativity from the self, then the self must seek them out and "privatize" them. After all, writes painter-critic Okamoto Tarō, in echoes of Ruskin and William Morris, viewing or listening or reading also can be creative processes. Creating does not simply mean creating *things*, objects with a market value. "The complete professional separation of savoring, viewing, and creating spells the decay of art," writes Okamoto. "In the modern arts there is no division into specialist, layman, amateur—just as there are no 'specialists' in the business of existence."

"Life is art" says the first of Perfect Liberty's Twenty-one Precepts. "The whole life of the individual is a continuous succession of self-expressions," says the second. Third is "The individual is a manifestation of God," and Fourth that "We suffer if we do not manifest ourselves." PL members meet each morning to exchange "artistic experiences" and pledge themselves to an artistic day. As one PL tract puts it:

> When inspired expressions are made, man always feels good, regardless of how difficult their processes may be. Toil itself becomes a great pleasure and joy. The frame of mind after the goal has been achieved is of course pleasant, but compared with the pleasure and fun experienced in the midst of the process, it resembles the taste of what one has thoroughly relished and enjoyed, like chewing-gum after it has been chewed thoroughly.

Self-development provokes special complications for the *deuxième sexe*. The Japanese woman has a world reputation for subservience, and she is not immune to the self-flattery of believing that she can out-sacrifice males. But for all its charms the role is painful to many incumbents. In postwar opinion surveys an overwhelming majority of Japanese women answer "yes" when asked if they would rather have been born male; the female suicide rate is well above that in Western nations. Spokeswomen insist that despite present legal and constitutional equality, the role never will be a satisfying one until they feel free and equal in fact. What they seem to hunger for is not complete sex desegregation so much as a mutual security pact that would stave off further Thurberian struggles while at the same time guaranteeing more psychic *Lebensraum*. As the young woman journalist Tabuse Mitsuko puts it:

It is often said that the happiness or unhappiness of a woman's whole life is decided as her husband wishes. But it seems to me that letting a woman's desires for growth be encouraged or restricted by her husband is an old-fashioned way of doing things. However the husband is regarded, there is not a little opposition to the idea that he can pull the human individual he calls wife into whatever shape he fancies. This does not mean that we should be conscious of males vs. females in all things. But it does mean that even though a couple are man and wife it is not proper for either to unduly intrude upon the time and pleasures which give vigor to the other's life. The age has gone that thought it a virtue for a wife to be a kind of ancillary to her husband. The idea that it is best for a wife to live under the direction of her husband would drive us women further and further into retreat.

Nozomi

Wartime defeat and the subsequent Occupation brought Japan a multiple American revolution. It brought a wave of GIs and their dependants who provided a free home demonstration of American material culture and social institutions. It brought in General MacArthur, a charismatic leader—"the Emperor couldn't have picked a better man" was the current quip—and an idealistic staff that insisted upon democratic reforms. And it brought more metaphorically but no less importantly a slaying of the primal fatherhood of the past. The Japanese did not lack moments of democratic fervor and experimentation in the late nineteenth and early twentieth centuries. But even the sweeping changes of the Meiji period are generally regarded as a "restoration" (the word favored by Western historians) or more literally, a "renovation." And down to 1945 vertical social ties continued to hold overwhelming prominence. The vertical ties have not disappeared in Japan any more than in the West. The Japanese have not lost all of the "faith in hierarchy" that so impressed Ruth Benedict; there is no need to overstate the case. But the postwar generation, now beginning to take up leadership positions, is convinced that whatever mass democracy may come to be it can never come to be a renewal of the vertical society.

What will happen in a decade or two when the postwar generation is in command? asks Professor Fukutake Tadashi of himself. His answer shows both a sense of revolution *accompli* and of problems left unsettled:

> Though it is true that men grow conservative as they advance in age, becoming more and more like the prewar type, there is a limit to such social selection. However reactionary the policy which may be followed in the fu-

181

ture, such a policy can never reinstitute a prewar Japan. Likewise, postwar men cannot be changed into men with the same social character as the prewar type or kept confined in the traditional pattern of social groups.

. . . It is futile to attempt to force the farmers, who had once borne the impact of Japan's industrial progress, to return to a physiocratic ideology and reconcile themselves to an indigent subsistence, thereby compelling them to bear again a cost which ought to be borne by a social policy. If an attempt is made to frustrate the laborers' consciousness of their right to live, it will only boomerang to make that consciousness stronger. What is necessary is to find the way in which agriculture can survive as a profitable enterprise and the laborers can expect the improvement of their living standard and can feel a real willingness to work. For the middle class also, ways and means must be established to keep the old middle class organized so as to insure small business a stable footing and also to guarantee the security of management and of employes. The new middle class, too, must be enabled to restore its "manhood" through the medium of its own autonomous organization if it is not to be disillusioned about the hoped-for rise in its level of consumption.

This does not mean that individualism is rampant, although the self is urged to be strong. Rather it means a search for new forms of democratic grouping (such as clubs and circles) and for greater equality within the old forms. As Y. Scott Matsumoto concludes from a study of postwar opinion polls, "Collectivity orientations remain predominant in the family, in occupational ties, in labor unions, in village life, and in politics. Where attitudinal changes are occurring, they are shifting from the collectivity orientations based on hierarchal doctrines, paternal authoritarianism, and lineal ancestry toward collectivity orientations based on collateral ties, peer-groups, and egalitarian views."

Beyond this, however, aims of a more concrete sort are not easy to formulate. I doubt that this is peculiarly Japanese, for I am inclined to agree with E. H. Carr when he points out (in *The New Society*) that even in the West with its democratic heritage, industrial mass democracy is something that does not need to be defended so much as discovered. To after-hours man this means that no one should be allowed to "unduly intrude" upon his time and pleasures. Yet his free access to them obviously is limited by time, money, and social ties. Japanese critics seem as sensitive to these restrictions as do their Western colleagues. In their excesses of complaint they sometimes are unrealistic. But the very bitterness of their sense of "poverty amid plenty" bespeaks the essence of modern frustration at approaching the shores of Cockaigne and being excluded for lack of a visa.

This, then, is the moral dilemma of after-hours man. He wants the security and comfort of a stable occupation (preferably salaried). He wants the maturity and emotions of parenthood and marriage (preferably for love). He wants a sense of "self-direction." Yet he wants none of these to be throttled by what now seem mere "accidents" of station, craft, residence, or sex. It cannot be done without some manner of submission to big government, big business, mass communications, mass society. A simple reassertion of older forms of groupishness is insufficient. A cynical submission at work in order to be free in leisure is unbalanced. But the submission should be as honorable as was that of Ninomiya.

For this as for any active dilemma there is no simple, stable resolution; one can express it better than explain it. The dilemma appears in miniature in Japanese concern over what men do on their way home from work. For the salaryman or the industrial worker this is the interval of the day most disputed between the two places where he spends the greater part of his life. He sleeps and eats at home; usually arises in the morning and goes directly to work; but the after-work interval is less fixed. American white-collar men have their customary after-hours cocktail, and blue-collar men their customary glass of beer. But "stopping off" seems even more common in Japan—or so, at least, the Japanese like to think. In the Tokyo University survey cited earlier, 64 per cent of metropolitan Tokyo men said they do "stop off," although frequency was not asked. In another survey of 1,108 metropolitan salarymen, a similar 31.1 per cent said they *never* "stop off." Of the 68.9 per cent who do, 26.9 per cent stop about once a week, 14.1 per cent twice, 13 per cent thrice, 9.2 per cent four times, and a big-spender fraction of 0.9 per cent stop off every day. No doubt many factors are involved, but some of the more crucial are these:

First, demands from the firm and from associates for postwork socializing. Perhaps this is no stronger than in the United States; it surely is no weaker. There are company parties, "contacts" to be entertained; office partners wanting to gripe about the boss. They also have overtones of masculinity, since women are rarely invited—except waitresses and entertainers. And the man who refuses to join the party risks scorn as a "homing pigeon" or less politely as "being sat on by his wife's behind."

Second, while complaints of the alienation of modern work are too often overdone, surely there is truth in them. And any man is likely to have days when he seeks some kind of change-of-pace or "restoration of actorness" through drinking, dancing, gambling, or simply strolling the streets. (In the Tokyo University survey, about half of those who said they do "stop off" said they don't have a particular place in mind but simply ramble.)

Third, lack of private automobiles and superhighways may mean that the average bus-and-subway commuter is more vulnerable to casual opportunities for a pick-me-up while awaiting the 5:10. At any rate this is one of the reasons given by the Canon Camera Corporation in urging its employes—many of whom live in a company tract —to pool their resources and buy a car for every four or five households. The news weeklies picked this up as a "GHQ movement." The GHQ means "go home quickly," not the Occupation's General Headquarters, twitted the weeklies; and the boss is not MacArthur but your wife.

Four, there are pressures from home. Quite apart from his own desires to be a good husband and father, the salaryman is likely to find his tied-down wife urging him to "at least be around the house" after hours, even though she may have no specific chores to ask of him. Furthermore, as Japanese writers sometimes point out, the postwar salaryman who has married at his choice a companionable and educated wife may find it much less stimulating to frolic with brassy and ignorant bar-girls.

Fifth, nevertheless, there still is a strong tradition of entertaining outside the home. The West has heard a great deal about the more extreme manifestations of this in the form of the geisha and the "flower and willow world" of the gay quarters. The geisha has become too classicized and too costly for most men except when they are using expense-account funds. And prostitution was outlawed in 1958, although as one Japanese reporter wrote recently, a good deal of "under the counter" prostitution remains. Furthermore the "hundred-yen salaryman" can find the same enjoyments in more modernized form—whether he seeks liaison or simply a moment of flirtation—with a bar-girl or cabaret "hostess" (*hosu-tesu*). This is especially important when out with fellow males. However companionable a wife may be, she is not likely to be capable of easy conversation in mixed company. She may act as "waitress" if one brings a few companions home to drink; she is not likely to join the fun. Cocktail parties have been held in the upper circles of Japanese society since the 1920's; and the idea of installing a "home bar" flits across the dreams of many salarymen today, but as yet only the *nouveau* is likely to consummate the purchase. American-style partying is held out as a model for scrutiny, though, as in this utopian excerpt from a news weekly:

> Their parties too, unlike Japanese ones, are extremely emancipated. The purpose of a party is to assemble a group of people who don't know each other very well and to expand the scope of their social ties.
>
> Like the theater or baseball "nighters," parties also begin after a short rest, in the home at about 8:00 or 8:30. The children go to bed at 7:00. If there is no one to stay with them, for a dollar an hour you hire a "baby sitter," i.e. a child-watcher. With one phone call you can get a high-school girl who does this as a spare-time job. The Americans' way of thinking is that children should live with children, parents with parents, that it is not good for children to be sacrificed to parents nor for parents to be sacrificed to children.
>
> If husband and wife do not get out together they feel inferior at a party. Wives also are extremely energetic about gaining education. It's the wives who are first aware of Kennedy's new policies or the latest best-sellers.
>
> In Japan the wife is nailed into the home and has few topics in common with her husband. This is the primary reason why her idol and master returns so slowly.

We can see all of these competing elements—wife, peers, ambitions, enjoyment—woven together in Japanese gray-flannel fiction. A good example is an hour-long drama called *Nozomi* ("Hopes"), which was broadcast over NHK television in July, 1960. The resolutions it offers seem to me representative of mainstream Japanese after-hours thinking.

Nozomi depicts the multiple fates of the salarymen. It centers about a husband and wife, childless, both in their mid-thirties. He is employed in the accounting section of a bank, she works for another firm as a Comptometer operator. In the opening scene she is frying eggs for his breakfast. As soon as his meal is ready, she rushes away, saying she must be at work early but extracting from him a promise to come home from work directly today.

At the office that morning the section chief is cleaning off his desk, announcing that he is retiring. A buddy who works next to the husband suggests that everyone in the office take the chief for a farewell party after work. But the husband demurs, mentioning his promise; the man opposite has a previous engagement; the girl at the next desk snaps that it is impudent to even suggest that she should go along. The buddy stands and glowers, "What's wrong with all of you? Don't you have any human feeling?"

As the husband and buddy are lunching, an acquaintance drifts by and asks if they have seen the new section chief? He is even younger than you two. The two of them fall glum, remarking that now they have no hope for advancement, they will be obliged to slog away at the same desks until retirement. The retiring section chief also fares badly. After 38 years with the firm, he still must wait outside the president's office all day in order to say farewell. Finally he is ushered in just before 4:00

P.M. The president absently reads him a certificate of thanks, interrupting to bark orders to an assistant; then walks out without further ceremony. The old man is reduced to walking to the assistant's office and begging for a mailing tube in which to preserve the certificate.

The husband relents, agreeing to accompany the buddy and the old chief for a few drinks. At a bar, in his cups, the old man laments that he has nothing to hope for after retirement. His pension and bonus will evaporate overnight, for he must use them to send his sons to college. He will have no choice but to seek a job somewhere, an underpaid bookkeeper in some small shop. If it ever becomes clear that you won't be promoted, he warns the two younger men, then get out at once. Once I had hopes, but then a younger man was made president over me. So go to night school and get yourself a CPA, be independent. But get out and do what you really want to do, or else life is over as quickly and as flatly as the foam in this beer glass.

The old man is seen off in a taxi, and the buddy urges that the husband continue the evening. The husband agrees to phone his wife and tell her that he will be late. All right dear, she says, enjoy yourself, but don't get sotted and hurt yourself falling out of a cab. The two visit several bars and cabarets. The buddy confesses that he is about to resign from the firm and take an executive position with a company that is building an electric power project in Burma. There is a position open for you, too, he says; so quit this boring bank and come with me. Think of it—money, adventure, the jungle, Burma! The husband is uncertain, but promises to go. As he is dancing with a hostess she accuses him of being a school-teacher, he is so restrained. Nonsense! he shouts, I work in the jungles of Burma, you know, guns, hunting and

all that. The buddy (still a bachelor) and another hostess are growing amorous, so the husband decides to return home, shooing off a streetwalker en route.

His wife is slumped over the table with an abacus as
he arrives. He flings his arms about, shouting that he will
damned well do as he pleases. He is about to tell her of
Burma and his promise when she says that she is preg-
nant, that she had left early this morning because she
wanted to see her doctor. She pleads that this time she
be allowed to keep the child. "This may be my last
chance." The husband begins to sober. "The important
thing is to take care of your health . . . it isn't that I
don't want children . . ." We have put it off for eight
years because of money, she says, but tonight I have been
figuring: if you continue to work regularly we will have
your retirement bonus just at the time our child will be
ready for college.

In a flashback the husband sees himself in the bar,
his buddy pounding him on the back and shouting in
English "Be Ambitious! Be Ambitious!" The wife
fondles a doll left behind by the child of a friend who
had visited that evening. The husband, sober, sits quietly
on the mats and says yes, from now on the child will be
his hope.

こたつでテレビを見る 健

8. *Between Arcadia*
and Utopia

The third generation stands on the side of the common people. We look at the West, and even at Asia and Africa, with the eye of the common man. For instance, we do not want to meet Mr. Nehru in a cool, quiet room to talk over politics or philosophy. We prefer to be in the baked and disease-ridden streets and view Mr. Nehru from there with love and hate, trust and suspicion. It is the same with our "hybrid culture." We are disgusted by it but it is ours and we have no alternative but to start from where we are. Our third generation suffers, but we feel that something extraordinarily different, strong and great will probably emerge from this hybrid culture.

ODA MAKOTO

Reprise

A century of struggle with industry and democracy has not converted Japan from an agrarian arcadia into an industrial utopia. Perhaps we can say of the industrial Japan of today as Sir George Sansom did of the agrarian Japan of Genroku, that it is "a happy society as human societies go." I think many Japanese would tend to agree with this—granting the uncertainties of a label such as "happiness." At the very least they would renounce any desire to re-enter the "dark valleys" of the feudal past. This is not to ignore the unhappiness, the inequalities, the inhumanities that are manifest. They would have to be reckoned with in any attempt to *evaluate* present-day Japanese ways of living. I have not dwelt upon them because my aim has been more limited. I have sought to clarify the transformations that modernity has wrought upon the Japanese search for enjoyment. In so doing I hope to serve those who strive to put into words for the sake of all of us the human meaning of the fact that in the modern milieu we are all at the same time workers and aristocrats.

The changes in Japanese life over the past hundred years have been multiple and pervasive, whether we examine them in the macrocosm of the great society or in the microcosm of a region such as Anchiku. Many of these changes had Western precedents and bear Western labels—even a Japanese illiterate now knows several hundred Anglo words. Tokugawa Japan had many similarities to feudal Europe, and perhaps was favorably "pre-adapted" to modernization along Western lines. In any event the past century has brought Japanese society and culture closer than ever to the West in form as well as in function. Nevertheless there continue to be customs and values and social forms such that the configuration is uniquely and characteristically Japanese. It is a Japanese modernism and not simply a Western one. Unless we see both of these facts at once we cannot begin to understand it, much less evaluate it.

I have chosen to view the impact of modernization through the transformations in one aspect of life, that of the after hours. Coördinated and standardized schedules were not absent from a civilization so complex as that of Tokugawa Japan. But today in a Japan with a trebled population, with mass production and distribution and consumption, with "instant" mass communications, the demands of standardized scheduling touch every life every day. The felt discontents of today may result partly from an increase in the after hours, although the amount of increase tends to be overstated. More likely the discontents result from the difficulties of adjusting to the changed rhythms of life that have arisen in the everyday behavioral environment in response to the demands of mass industry and mass democracy. Out of this process are emerging new rhetorics of time-use, such as the vacation and the "circle," and new styles of individual and family living. The salaryman style is becoming one of the most widespread, and is felt to be best suited to the "mechanical" tempo of modern routine. As the style spreads, more and more people come to see—at least to sense—a division of daily living into spheres of work versus leisure or of family versus establishment. In recent years this feeling has been articulated in the idiom of "the leisure problem."

The century also has brought better health and longevity, an easing of drudgery, and a general sense of comfort to the Japanese. Ideals of material progress, social equality and social security have been growing in favor since 1868 and have predominated since 1945. At the same time that the social order is demanding greater conformity—perhaps as a response to this demand—people are voicing greater concern for the fate of the human individual. Western influences have played a part in this, but so too have the burgeoning complexity and interdependence found in all industrial civilizations. And although Ninomiya himself has become as submerged as Santayana's Last Puritan, the Ninomiya image continues to remind the Japanese that honorable self-denial and submission to the nexus remains possible.

We cannot begin to understand such a Japan or surmise its trends until we discard cherished images of the Japanese as poor and underdeveloped and still subject to Western tutelage. Japanese-Western differences in personal income or public welfare or military might are unmistakable. The point is that despite these differences the human problems which modernity has imposed upon the Japanese are overwhelmingly like those it has imposed upon Americans and Europeans. As an opposing self, Japan mirrors us in naked detail.

And Preview

By my lights the virtue of studying the Japanese after hours is not that they transport us to lotus-land but that they force us to scrutinize the self as in a well-lighted mirror. This should be the virtue of all ethnography, although too often the fate of ethnographic reporting is etherealization. An exotic society is easy to romanticize —or to reject. We can use it for wish-fulfillment; tell ourselves that if only our lives were more ritualized (like the Zuni), or our men more bold (like the Crow), or our women more graceful (like the Balinese). Or we can read of human variations and dismiss them as disgusting or perverse. We invite the ethnographer to tell us about human differences. We forget that he is also a watchdog: he guards the reality of the human context within which these differences take place. He warns us that to know the variations and ignore the contexts is to shy from facing humanity in its fullest dimensions.

The Japanese after hours show us human differences within a context that is anything but unfamiliar. One can romanticize it, of course, but Oda's "hybrid culture" is ours too. If we are disgusted by it, we must work from what we have. I doubt that we need more utopias and arcadias; I should be satisfied if we tried to live out the ones we have. Paul Goodman writes, "Finding a new ethics or esthetics . . . will not put us in a state of grace. Existence is not given meaning by importing into it a revelation from outside. The meaning is *there*, in more closely contacting the actual situation, the only situation that there is, whatever it is. As our situation is, closely contacting it would surely result in plenty of trouble and perhaps in terrible social conflicts, terrible opportunities and duties, during which we might learn something and at the *end* of which we might know something, even a new ethics; for it is in such conflicts that new ethics are discovered." An inescapable first step is to understand the context within which we must act.

By the end of the nineteenth century the Japanese had dispelled any shred of mystique that Europeans and Americans had a monopoly on industrial civilization. Today Japan also stands as a warning that Europeans and Americans are not peculiarly susceptible to the human problems of industrial civilization. It is conceivable that some new nation in Asia or Africa, building from radically different bases and profiting by the Western and Japanese experiments, may develop an industrial democracy untarnished by alienation, materialism, or "Coca-Cola culture." I doubt at the same time that I hope. From the instances of modernity *accompli*, I can hardly avoid the conclusion that these problems inhere in the industrial social order as we know it.

We need not fear modern civilization as a juggernaut. I only underline the familiar point that patterns of culture are not accidental assemblages. Industrial democracy is not only a complex form of culture, it forms a cultural complex. The process of modernization is not a cash-and-carry transaction. One does not load up in the Western or Japanese supermarket and simply walk away with the goods. They carry with them less visible but no less inescapable social forms and cultural values. As Georg Simmel writes, "from each point on the surface of existence—however closely attached to the surface alone—one may drop a sounding into the depth of the psyche so that all the most banal externalities of life finally are connected with the ultimate decisions concerning the meaning and style of life." I wonder if in their heart of hearts the leaders of Meiji Japan were not admitting this to themselves even at the same time that outwardly they were proclaiming an ability to graft Western techniques upon Eastern morals.

The implication is not that in another generation the world all will be dully Western; the Japanese have preserved a parochial identity, however "hybrid" it may seem to some. The implication is that in another generation the world all will encounter the problems now troubling both Japan and the West. If modern civilization is not inherently Western, neither are that civilization's discontents. As we watch our opposing selves in Asia and Africa cope with these discontents we shall come to know more about ourselves. But we shall also come to know more about others. For what better way to understand a man than to measure his reactions to the selfsame situation we face?

Notes

For each chapter I first suggest further readings, and then cite my sources of data, tables, and quotations. Each citation is given in full when first used but in abbreviated form when used subsequently.

Chapter 1

Our understanding of a people is continually being thwarted by alluring stereotypes we feel compelled to build out of fragments of information. The present Zen-colored image of Japan is a case in point. Notice the dismay of the Buddhist scholar Hanayama Shōyū, reflecting upon a year's stay at the Union Theological Seminary in New York. Even advanced seminarians there knew nothing of Buddhism *as a way of life*, he sighs, "the little they knew, based on books written in English by non-Japanese scholars, was restricted to the philosophical aspects of the subject." (From his "Buddhism for Americans," *Atlas* 5:6 [June, 1963] 364–365). And beloved Madame Butterfly was, after all, an American creation, even though Puccini later put Italian lyrics into her mouth. See the well-written sketch of American images of Japan and vice-versa in Robert S. Schwantes, *Japanese and Americans, A Century of Cultural Relations* (New York, 1955), esp. 9–39, "Eyes Across the Pacific."

Much has been written in recent years concerning the after hours in modern industrial society, but nearly all of it is limited to North Atlantic civilizations. To the general reader I commend David Riesman's *The Lonely Crowd: A Study of the Changing American Character* (New Haven, 1950, and later editions); and his essays collected in *Individualism Reconsidered* (Glencoe, 1954, and later editions). More recently Sebastian de Grazia in *Of Time, Work and Leisure* (New York, 1962) has written a popular summary of materials gathered by the Twentieth Century Fund. He strives too hard to be clever, but the book contains much useful material and an excellent bibliography.

On the academic frontier, sociologists have particularly been drawn to the study of leisure since early in the twentieth century. The most complete bibliography appears in the collection edited by Eric Larrabee and Rolf Meyersohn, *Mass Leisure* (Glencoe, 1958), pp. 389–419. There are recent monographs by Nels Anderson, *Work and Leisure* (Glencoe, 1961) and by Max Kaplan, *Leisure in America: A Social Inquiry* (New York and London, 1960). There are three general collections of essays and research reports: Larrabee and Meyersohn, *Mass Leisure*; its companion volume edited by Bernard Rosenberg and David Manning White, *Mass Culture, The Popular Arts in America* (Glencoe, 1957); and most recently Erwin O. Smigel (ed.), *Work and Leisure: A*

Contemporary Social Problem (New Haven, 1963). See also three special issues of different journals: "The Uses of Leisure," *American Journal of Sociology* 62:6 (May, 1957); "Recreation in the Age of Automation," *The Annals of the American Academy of Political and Social Science*, vol. 313 (September, 1957): and "Sociological Aspects of Leisure," *International Social Science Journal* 12:4 (1960). Finally, see the collection edited by Robert W. Kleemeier, *Aging and Leisure* (New York, 1961).

Those able to read Japanese will find a good compilation of materials and essays in Seikatsu Kagaku Chōsakai (hen), *Yoka, Nihonjin no Seikatsu Shisō* (Tokyo, 1961); and a bibliography of Japanese studies of the after hours from late Meiji onward in Satō Takeshi, "Saikin no taishū goraku, yoka no kenkyū," *Shisō* #431 (May, 1960), 113–130.

References

PAGE

1–The motto is from Lynn White, Jr., "The Changing Canons of Our Culture," pp. 301–316 in his *Frontiers of Knowledge in the Study of Man* (New York, 1956), p. 312.

6–Georges Friedmann speaks of "contemporary hedonism" in his "Leisure and Technological Civilization," *International Social Science Journal* 12:4 (1960), 509–521. Don Marquis' line is from "Archie Is Excited," *The Lives and Times of Archie and Mehitabel* (Garden City, 1935), p. 406.

7–For Katō Hidetoshi on *kaiteki* see his *Chūkan Bunka* (Tokyo, 1957).

8–Sapir's essay is available *in* David Mandelbaum (ed.), *Selected Writings of Edward Sapir* (Berkeley and Los Angeles, 1951), pp. 308–331.

11–On vernacular culture see Margaret Lantis, "Vernacular Culture," *American Anthropologist* 62 (1960), 202–216. Chamberlain's caution appears on page 2 of the 1902 edition of *Things Japanese*.

Chapter 2

The good Reverend Weston came into Anchiku over the hills from Karuizawa to the East in 1892 riding a bumpy rickshaw. During his forays about the valley he developed a long-term friendship with a Matsumoto innkeeper, complained sometimes

199

of attacks by newspaper reporters and constantly of attacks by fleas, dispensed quinine to ailing natives, always carried his own cocoa and marmalade but attempted to teach local bakers to prepare bread to his taste. His chatty accounts of his travels afford many sympathetic glimpses into Anchiku life a half century ago. See his *Mountaineering and Exploration in the Japanese Alps* (London, 1896) and *The Playground of the Far East* (London, 1918).

During these same years an Anchiku boy went to explore the artistic and bohemian wilds of Europe and America. Ogiwara Rokuzan, born in a Hotaka hamlet in 1879, was attracted to Christianity and then to Western art. He went to Paris in 1903 and for a time studied under Rodin, whose influence is obvious in many of his works. He returned to Tokyo in 1908 and died there in 1910. In 1958 a Rokuzan museum, built in the form of a brick chapel of northwest European style, was opened on the grounds of the Hotaka middle school.

I know of nothing written in Western languages that deals directly with Anchiku history, although the region occasionally is given passing mention. One Ariake folktale, "Yamura no Yasuke," has become a collector's favorite. It appears in numerous Japanese collections and has been translated into English twice: see Yanagida Kunio (translated by Fanny H. Mayer), *Japanese Folk Tales* (Tokyo, 1952), pp. 175–177; and Richard M. Dorson, *Folk Legends of Japan* (Rutland and Tokyo, 1962), pp. 81–83.

References

PAGE

13–The motto was contributed by Taibi, who is Dr. Akanuma Shigeyoshi, physician, poet, and gentleman, who opened his Ariake home to my family and me in 1959 and 1960.

25–Weston's remarks are from his *Playground*, pp. 140, 143, 144.

Chapter 3

The three families are drawn from field interviews. Their names are fictitious, as will be patent to anyone who knows the Japanese language. I have altered a few noncritical features to preserve anonymity.

For further information on the postwar salaryman see the

recent and detailed study by Ezra F. Vogel, *Japan's New Middle Class* (Berkeley and Los Angeles, 1963). There are useful sections in R. P. Dore's readable *City Life in Japan* (Berkeley and Los Angeles, 1958), and to a lesser extent in James G. Abegglen, *The Japanese Factory* (Glencoe, 1958).

Materials on the farmer are plentiful. In the 1950's the University of Michigan's Center for Japanese Studies sponsored several investigations of rural life. The most comprehensive report is that by R. K. Beardsley, J. W. Hall and R. E. Ward, *Village Japan* (Chicago, 1959) based upon an Okayama hamlet. A fishing community is depicted in Edward Norbeck's *Takashima, A Japanese Fishing Community* (Salt Lake City, 1954); and two different agricultural communities are contrasted in John B. Cornell and Robert J. Smith, *Two Japanese Villages* (Ann Arbor, Center for Japanese Studies, Occasional Papers no. 5, 1956). In addition to the Michigan studies, see three recent doctoral dissertations: Erwin H. Johnson, *Nagura Mura: An Historical Analysis of Persistence and Change in Community Structure* (Columbia University, 1961); Harumi Befu, *Hamlet in a Nation, the Place of Three Japanese Rural Communities in Their Broader Social Context* (University of Wisconsin, 1962); and James A. Hirabayashi, *The Relation Between National and Local Normative Systems, a Study of a Japanese Mountain Community* (Harvard University, 1963). Papers on specific topics are too numerous to list, but see the general sketch of recent rural transformations in Edward Norbeck's "Postwar Cultural Change and Continuity in Northeastern Japan," *American Anthropologist* 63 (1961), 297–321. On changes in farming itself see Tobata Sei'ichi's concise and pointed *An Introduction to Agriculture of Japan* (Tokyo, 1958); and for an exhaustive report on the land reforms including their prewar background see R. P. Dore, *Land Reform in Japan* (London, 1959).

The merchant is much less well reported. Dore's *City Life* is helpful for the postwar scene; and for the Tokugawa merchant one can turn to Charles D. Sheldon, *The Rise of the Merchant Class in Tokugawa Japan 1600–1868* (Association for Asian Studies Monographs, no. 5, 1958) or to bourgeois novels such as that by Ihara Saikaku (translated by G. W. Sargent), *The Japanese Family Storehouse* (Cambridge University Oriental Publications, no. 3, 1959). For an enjoyable discussion of the continuities between Tokugawa and modern townsmen see the essay by Robert J. Smith "Pre-industrial Urbanism in Japan: a Consideration of Multiple Traditions in a Feudal Society," *Economic Development and Cultural Change* 9:1 (October, 1960), 241–257.

References

PAGE

33–The motto is taken from Robert Redfield, *The Primitive World and Its Transformations* (Ithaca, 1953), p. 53.

34–Schumpeter's lines appear in *Capitalism, Socialism and Democracy* (3d edition, New York, 1951), p. ix.

37–C. Wright Mills *White Collar* (New York, 1951), p. ix.

47–Redfield from *Primitive World*, p. 57.

49–For further materials on social and technological changes in Japanese agriculture before 1868 see Thomas C. Smith's well-documented study *The Agrarian Origins of Modern Japan* (Stanford, 1959).

59–Smith from "Pre-industrial Urbanism," pp. 247–248.

Chapter 4

The chapter is not intended as a full-dress portrait of Japanese ideals but only as a sketch of those features most relevant to the search for enjoyment. I have cribbed energetically from the works of others, of which I recommend the following.

The tyro will do well to begin with Ruth Benedict's *The Chrysanthemum and the Sword* (Boston, 1946). It is the most balanced of the wartime studies of Japanese character, and by far the most readable. It has its faults, of course, and perhaps the best single corrective to it is in John W. Bennett and Michio Nagai, "The Japanese Critique of The Methodology of Benedict's *Chrysanthemum and the Sword*," *American Anthropologist*, 55 (1953), 404–411.

About the time that Benedict was writing, a Japanese scholar was completing a comparative study of thought ways among Japanese, Chinese, and Indians. It was published in Japanese in 1947 but only recently translated: Nakamura Hajime, *The Ways of Thinking of Eastern Peoples* (Tokyo, 1960). Nearly half of the translated edition is devoted to Japan. The translation leaves much to be desired, but the book is rich in insights.

Western research into Japanese ideals and values since Benedict's time has been less inclusive in scope but more exacting of detail and more self-conscious about methods of inference and proof. In his *Tokugawa Religion* (Glencoe, 1957), Robert N. Bellah attempts to apply a Max Weber-Talcott Parsons framework of theory to Japanese ideals in the Tokugawa period. Although he bases his analysis on pre-1868 materials, most of the general picture applies as well to later times. And although I find the book overly jargonistic, the evidence it presents for a Japanese "Protestant Ethic" is convincing, and Bellah's description of the Japanese values system is admirable. An interesting study by Y. Scott Matsumoto traces postwar trends in attitudes as manifested in public opinion surveys: *Contemporary Japan, The Individual and the Group* (Transactions of the American Philosophical Society 50: part 1, 1960).

Three anthologies contain useful papers. The most up-to-date is Robert J. Smith and Richard K. Beardsley (eds.), *Japanese Culture: Its Development and Characteristics* (Viking Fund Publications in Anthropology no: 34, 1962). The papers in Bernard S. Silberman's *Japanese Character and Culture* (Tucson, 1962) date from the 1950's and earlier. And five papers on Japan are included in Douglas G. Haring (ed.), *Personal Character and Cultural Milieu* (Syracuse, 1956, third ed.). Relevant materials appear in some sections of Charles W. Morris, *Varieties of Human Value* (Chicago, 1956), and of Jean Stoetzel, *Without the Chrysanthemum and the Sword: A Study of the Attitudes of Youth in Postwar Japan* (New York, 1955). For a survey of research done through 1960 see Edward Norbeck and George De Vos, "Culture and Personality: the Japanese," *in* F. L. K. Hsu (ed.), *Psychological Anthropology* (Homewood, 1961). Three important papers have been published since that time: William Caudill and Harry A. Scarr, "Japanese value orientations and culture change," *Ethnology* 1:1 (January, 1962), 53–91; George De Vos and Hiroshi Wagatsuma, "Value Attitudes Toward Role Behavior of Women in Two Japanese Villages," *American Anthropologist* 63:6 (December, 1961), 1204–1230; and Takeo Doi, "Amae—a Key Concept for Understanding Japanese Personality Structure," *Psychologia* 5 (1962):1–7. Some notes on Japanese research into the problem occur in Yamamoto Tatsuro, "Recent Studies on the Japanese National Character," unpublished ms., Wenner-Gren Foundation for Anthropological Research, 1962.

One should not overlook the prewar writers. They are out-of-date in some ways, but they may be the more valuable precisely because their biases stand out so sharply. Much can be learned from Lafcadio Hearn, incurable romantic that he is. Especially useful is his *Japan, An Attempt at Interpretation* (New York, 1904). And of many others I might mention, I am especially fond of the charm and wit of Nitobe Inazo as he explains himself and his countrymen in *Bushido, the Soul of Japan* (Tokyo, 1935).

References

PAGE

68–The motto from Ōgiya Shōzō, "Tanoshimi no hakken," pp. 5–19 *in Seikatsu no Tanoshimi*, pp. 14–15.

69–The Ninomiya homily and the quotation both are from Tanabe Shin'ichi, "Nihon no seikatsu shisō to sono henkaku," pp. 127–153 *in Yoka*, pp. 129–130. For Ninomiya the man, as distinguished from the image, see Robert C. Armstrong, *Just Before the Dawn: The Life and Work of Ninomiya Sontoku* (New York, 1912), and Ishiguro Tada'atsu, *Ninomiya Sontoku: His Life and Evening Talks* (Tokyo, 1955).

70–1–Clyde Kluckhohn from his "Common Humanity and Diverse Cultures," pp. 245–284 *in* Daniel Lerner (ed.), *The Human Meaning of the Social Sciences* (New York, 1959), p. 247.

73–Huston Smith, *The Religions of Man* (New York, 1959), p. 76. Nakamura, *The Ways of Thinking*, p. 527 and p. 311.

74–De Vos, from his review of Bellah's *Tokugawa Religion* in *American Anthropologist* 60 (1958):401–402.

76–I have put Pelzel's paradigm into my own phrasing; he developed the idea during lectures on Japanese and Chinese social organization, Harvard University, spring term, 1959.

77–Lord Avebury [Sir John Lubbock], *The Pleasures of Life* (London, 1889–1890), Chaps. 1 and 2.

79–See Caudill, "Around the Clock Patient Care in Japanese Psychiatric Hospitals: the Role of the Tsukisoi," *American Sociological Review* 26:2 (1961), 204–214. Benedict, *The Chrysanthemum and the Sword*, p. 177.

80–Nakamura, *The Ways of Thinking*, p. 551: Benedict, *The Chrysanthemum and the Sword*, p. 192.

82–I am thinking of Homans' *Social Behavior: Its Elementary Forms* (New York, 1961).

85–Pelzel from his "Lectures on Japanese Sociology," Department of State, Foreign Service Institute, September, 1954 (mimeographed), p. 22.

86–Nitobe, *Bushido*, p. 37.

92–3–The table is adapted from Okabe Keimi, "Goraku shikō to seikatsu yōshiki no henka—sono shinrigakuteki imi no rikai wo chūshin to shite," *Shisō* no. 431 (May, 1960): 51–59. Okabe does not specify the exact number of male respondents; presumably it is about half of the 914 completed interviews. For related materials see Chapter 7, and the books mentioned above by Morris, Matsumoto, and Stoetzel.

Chapter 5

One of the best sources on Japanese calendrics and time concepts still is Ernest Clement's "Japanese Calendars," *Transactions of the Asiatic Society of Japan* 30 (1902):1–32. Clement republished substantially the same materials in "Father Time in Japan or Japanese Calendars," *American Antiquity* 25 (1903):25–36, 247–254. More recent but less comprehensive is the section in the handbook compiled by the Japanese National Commission for UNESCO *Japan: Its Land, People, and Culture* (Tokyo, 1958), pp. 954–967. Robert J. Smith offers some pertinent comments in "Japan: the Later Years of Life and the Concept of Time," pp. 95–100 *in* Kleemeier, *Aging and Leisure*. I know of no general study of the changes in time reckoning from Tokugawa to Meiji; Clement touches upon it briefly, and there are suggestions in Yanagida Kunio, *Japanese Manners and Customs in the Meiji Era* (Tokyo, 1957).

One has to build up a picture of the daily round from fiction, biography, and ethnography. Of the latter, see especially "The Routine of Household Life" in a Honshu mountain village, in Cornell and Smith, *Two Japanese Villages*, pp. 165–172; and for a farming hamlet in Okayama, "Household Work Routines" in Beardsley, Hall, and Ward, *Village Japan*, pp. 228–232.

The yearly round is reported in much greater detail. For the

Meiji era see Yanagida, *Japanese Manners*, Chapter 10. For a prewar village in Kyushu, John F. Embree's *Suye Mura: A Japanese Village* (Chicago, 1939), Chapters 2 and 8. And for postwar communities the relevant portions of *Two Japanese Villages*, *Village Japan*, *Takashima*, and Dore's *City Life*. Numerous books and pamphlets have been devoted to the annual festival cycle, but most of them are intended to tickle the fancy of the jaded tourist. One of the better ones is Uenoda Setsuo *Calendar of Annual Events in Japan* (Tokyo, 1954).

The most accessible discussion of the postwar labor codes occurs in Solomon B. Levine, *Industrial Relations in Postwar Japan* (Urbana, 1958), Chapter 6. But also see various remarks in Abegglen's *The Japanese Factory*.

Those who can read Japanese naturally have much more material to choose from: For calendrics a good place to start is Nōda Tada'aki, *Koyomi* (Tokyo, 1957), and Wada Shōshū, "Koyomi to nenjū gyōji," *Nihon Minzokugaku Taikei* 7 (1959):17–66, both of which suggest numerous other sources. The Japanese folklorists have been rather indifferent to the daily and weekly cycles, but they have assembled a massive body of data on the annual round. To break into this literature the newcomer should begin with one of the handbooks and proceed from there. I am partial to the four-volume set prepared by the Nihon Minzokugaku Kyōkai, *Nihon Shakai-Minzoku Jiten* (Tokyo, 1952–1960). But see also the single-volume compendia of Nishitsunoi Masayoshi (hen), *Nenjū Gyōji Jiten* (Tokyo, 1958), and of the Minzokugaku Kenkyūsho (hen), *Minzokugaku Jiten* (Tokyo, 1951). The latter has been translated into English for the Kentucky Microcard Series under the title *Japanese Folklore Dictionary* (Kentucky Microcards, Series A, Modern Language Series, no. 18).

The one good Japanese source I have found for daily and weekly rounds in the Tokugawa period is Mitamura Engyō's "Jikoku no hanashi," in his *Ichi'i no Fūzoku* (Tokyo, 1958), pp. 189–214. In the modern era the Japanese have taken to feeling their social pulse as energetically as have men in the West. There are many surveys of working hours and time uses, most of them sponsored by interested parties such as labor and education bureaus, advertising agencies, mass communications media, and so on. For a brief introduction to some of these studies see Kojima Wabito's "Nihonjin no yoka jikan," pp. 27–62 *in Yoka*.

Utsumi Yoshio's *Rōdō Jikan no Rekishi* (Tokyo, 1959) is bent by Marxian attitudes but contains much material on the shorter-hours movements.

References

PAGE

95–The motto is from a tract by Marx's son-in-law Paul La-fargue, *The Right to Be Lazy, Being a Refutation of the "Right to Work" of 1848;* excerpts reprinted on pp. 105–118 *in* Larrabee and Meyersohn, *Mass Leisure,* p. 105.

96–Mumford's dictum from *Technics and Civilization* (New York, 1934), p. 14. On Roman timekeeping see Jerome Carcopino *Daily Life in Ancient Rome* (Penguin ed., 1956), pp. 149–154.

97–Drucker from *The New Society: The Anatomy of Industrial Order* (New York, 1950), pp. 4–5. Wilensky's rebuttal occurs in "The Uneven Distribution of Leisure: the Impact of Economic Growth on 'Free Time,'" pp. 107–145 *in* Smigel, *Work and Leisure.* De Grazia's is in his *Of Time, Work, and Leisure,* especially Chapter 3.

99–Conrad Arensberg from "The Community as Object and as Sample," *American Anthropologist* 63:2 (1961), 241–264, p. 252.

101–Sjoberg, *The Preindustrial City* (Glencoe, 1960), p. 210. Saikaku's line is quoted by Mitamura, *Ichi'i no Fūzoku,* p. 191.

102–Mitamura, *op. cit.* For African troubles in adjusting to a three-meal day see Melville J. Herskovits "The Problem of Adapting Societies to New Tasks," pp. 89–112, *in* Bert F. Hoselitz (ed.), *The Progress of Underdeveloped Areas* (Chicago, 1952), especially pp. 98–99.

104–On the "Mamma's Nine O'Clock Movement" see "Kāchan kuji made. . . ," *Shūkan Yomiuri,* May 1, 1960, pp. 10–11. The time-conscious American telephone operator is described on p. 39 of "Tenkai suru Nihonkei rejā būmu," *Shūkan Tōyō Keizai,* January 7, 1961, pp. 28–40.

105–Edward T. Hall's concepts on timekeeping appear in *The Silent Language* (Garden City, 1959), Chapter 1. The comparative study of dreams is reported in Richard M. Griffith, Otoya Miyagi, and Akira Tago "The Universality of Typical Dreams: Japanese vs. American," *American Anthropologist*

60 (1958):1173–1179. Yokoi's novel is discussed by R. P. Dore in "Agricultural Improvement in Japan: 1870–1900," *Economic Development and Cultural Change* 9:1 (October, 1960), especially on pp. 79–80. Of many reports by the Women's and Minors' Bureau, see particularly *Shufu no Jiyū-jikan ni Kansuru Ishiki Chōsa* (Fujin Kankei Shiryō Shiriizu Chōsa Shiryō, no. 28, Tokyo, 1959).

108–Kaempfer from the 1906 English translation of his *The History of Japan* [1690–1692] (Glasgow, 1906), vol. II, pp. 21–22.

109–For the Economic Planning Board survey see Nihon Seisansei Hombu, *Dai-sanji Sangyō ni Kansuru Shōhisha Dōkō Chōsa* (Tokyo, 1961, 4 vols. mimeo.). See also Rōdōsho Fujin-shōnen Kyoku, *Nenshō Rōdōsha Yoka Jōkyō Chōsa* (Shonen Rōdō Chōsa Shiryō, no. 47, Tokyo, 1960); and Odabashi Tadahisa "Chūshō kigyō rōdō to rekuriēshon," *Toshi Mondai* 51:2 (February, 1960) 19–31.

110–On the Western configurations of the weekly round see Margaret Mead, "The Pattern of Leisure in Contemporary American Culture," *The Annals*, no. 313 (September, 1957) 11–15; reprinted in Larrabee and Meyersohn, *Mass Leisure*, pp. 10–15. For a case study of an attempt to induce workers in a California aircraft plant to abandon their accustomed rounds see Rolf Meyersohn, "Changing Work and Leisure Routines," pp. 97–106 in Smigel, *Work and Leisure*.

111–Figures on prewar rural rest days from Namiki Masayoshi, *Nōson wa Kawaru* (Tokyo, 1960), pp. 61–66. Embree describes such rest days for a Kyushu village in the 1930's in *Suye Mura*, pp. 264–267.

113–Confucius from Legge's translation of *The Li Ki*, Sacred Books of the East, vol. 28, p. 167. Suzuki as quoted by Sakurai Takeo in the column "Nōson wo aruite," *Asahi Shimbun*, March 13, 1960.

114–Matsushita's address is quoted and discussed in "Matsushita Kōnosuke no nichiyō nibai ron," *Shūkan Bunshun*, March 14, 1960, pp. 11–17. Matsushita achieved immortalization on the cover of *Time* for the issue of February 23, 1962, which visualizes him on pp. 93–97 as a "Japanese Henry Ford." The prize essay appears in full in the Utsunomiya, *Tochigi Shimbun*, October 26, 1960.

115–Hutton Webster *Rest Days, A Sociological Study* (University of Nebraska Studies, vol. 9; Lincoln, 1911).

116–Tanizaki's doleful lines are from pp. 51–52 of "In Praise of Shadows," as translated by E. G. Seidensticker, *Japan Quarterly* 1:1 (October–December, 1954), 46–52. However, in his postwar novels Tanizaki's characters, at least, are as eager as other Japanese for chrome-and-plastic modernity.

117–Emile Durkheim *The Elementary Forms of the Religious Life* (London, 1915), pp. 10–11.

118–The study of the uses of different calendars is reported in Meishin Chōsa Kyōgikai (hen), *Nihon no Zokushin 1: Meishin no Jittai* (Tokyo, 1949), pp. 2–9.

122–Sony Corporation as reported by *Shūkan Asahi*, October 14, 1960, p. 78. The letter to the *Tokyo Shimbun* was translated and reprinted in the *Asahi Evening News*, January 11, 1961. For a discussion of English attempts to deal with the problem of staggered holidays see J. A. R. Pimlott, *The Englishman's Holidays* (London, 1947), Chapter 13.

Chapter 6

The classical Japanese arts and entertainments have been described and analyzed many times, so that books are plentiful on kabuki, nō, sumō, tea-ceremony, haiku, etc. Their modern—and usually more popular—avatars are less well known to the West, although flamboyant forms often catch the attention of reporters and travelers. Of recent reportage, see the special issue of *Holiday* 30:4 (October, 1961); the special issue of *Show* 3:5 (May, 1963); a photo-story in color "Japan's Dazzle After Dark," *Life*, February 23, 1962; and A. M. Rosenthal, "*La Dolce Vita* Along the Ginza," *New York Times Magazine*, October 14, 1962. There are some fine photographs and pertinent remarks in Donald Keene, *Living Japan* (Garden City, 1959), Chapter 9. More personal and often very witty is D. J. Enright's appreciation *The World of Dew* (London, 1955). On movies see Joseph L. Anderson and Donald Ritchie, *The Japanese Film* (New York, 1959). And for translations of some Japanese studies of popular fiction, movies, comic strips and so on, Katō Hidetoshi, *Japanese Popular Culture* (Rutland and Tokyo, 1959). Humbler everyday activities can be glimpsed from ethnographic field reports, of which Chapter 15 of Dore's *City Life* is especially pertinent. There are useful materials in almost every issue of *The Japan Quarterly*.

For an introduction to Japanese high life in the Genroku period I commend Howard Hibbett's *The Floating World in Japanese Fiction* (New York, 1959). But see also Charles J. Sheldon, *The Rise of the Merchant Class in Tokugawa Japan* (Monographs of the Association for Asian Studies, no. 5, 1958), Chapter 5; Takekoshi Yosoburo's *The Economic Aspects of the History of the Civilization of Japan* (3 volumes, London, 1930), vol. 2, Chapter 46; and relevant sections of Sir George B. Sansom's *The Western World and Japan* (New York, 1950).

In the examples from Anchiku the names are fictitious, except for that of Mr. Yamada Hiroshi of Otari. My thanks to Mr. Yamada and to several other innkeepers who remain unnamed, for enlightening me about resort-keeping. The reader may find it interesting to contrast the development of Otari with that of the more lavish hostelry (not an onsen, however) which Oliver Statler portrays in his *Japanese Inn* (New York, 1961). For an amusing fictional account of a Japanese outing see Thomas Raucat, *The Honorable Picnic* (New York, 1927).

I thank the ladies of the Dahlia Group, who graciously allowed me to attend one of their meetings, and who permitted me to make a copy of the club's minute-book. For a more systematic discussion of associations and their roles in Japanese life see Edward Norbeck, "Common-Interest Associations in Rural Japan," pp. 73–85 *in* Smith and Beardsley, *Japanese Culture*; and the same author's unpublished manuscript "Associations and Democracy in Japan," 1963.

References

PAGE

124–The motto from Kaempfer's *History*, vol. 2, p. 21.

125–Sansom, *The Western World and Japan*, p. 197.

126–Singer from p. 106 of his "The Great Tradition of Hinduism in the City of Madras," *in* Charles Leslie (ed.), *The Anthropology of Folk Religion* (New York, 1960). Yoshida as quoted in the Osaka edition of the *Asahi Shimbun*, January 21, 1961. The U. S. government report is quoted in W. A. Dobriner *The Suburban Community*

(New York, 1958), p. 259. For a similar line of argument see Joffre Dumazedier "Current Problems of the Sociology of Leisure," *International Social Science Journal*, 12, 4 (1960) 522–531.

127–Hallowell "The Self and Its Behavioural Environment," *Explorations* no. 2 (April, 1954); reprinted as Chapter 4 of his *Culture and Experience* (Philadelphia, 1955).

128–Malinowski from *Argonauts of the Western Pacific* (London, 1922), p. 209.

129–de Grazia "The uses of time," pp. 113–154 *in* Kleemeier *Aging and Leisure*, pp. 142–143. Hall, *The Silent Language, passim*.

130–1–Tanikawa "*Nagara-zoku* no tanoshimi," pp. 179–189 *in Seikatsu no Tanoshimi*, pp. 181–182.

132–Historical data on annual leaves from Harada Toshiaki "Matsuri no hi to toki," *Nihon Minzokugaku Taikei* 8: 231–248.

133–4–Figures on travel from *Nihon Keizai Shimbun*, February 17, 1961, and *Kyoto Shimbun*, March 13, 1961.

134–Pimlott, *The Englishman's Holidays*, p. 238.

135–Walpole as quoted by Pimlott, pp. 35–36. Description of the "New World" from the English-language *Mainichi*, June 22, 1960.

136–Quotation translated from Takahisa Jinnosuke, "Jo," *in* Shimodaira Hiroe, *Shinshū Onsen Annai* (Nagano, 1942), pp. 1–2.

137–On the changing role of the Imperial Household see Ishida Takeshi, "Popular Attitudes Toward the Japanese Emperor," *Asian Survey* 2:2 (April, 1962), 29–39.

145–Embree, *Suye Mura*, p. 170.

153–Minami Hiroshi, *Masu Komyunikēshon Nyūmon, Gendai wo Shihai Suru Mono* (Tokyo, 1960), pp. 203–204. For a handy summary of the two activities surveys see *Yoka*, pp. 48–54.

154–On napping American farmers see John E. Ross and L. R. Bastian, *Time-use Patterns and Communications Activities of Wisconsin Farm-Families* (University of Wisconsin Department of Agricultural Journalism Bulletin no. 8, Madison, 1958).

211

Chapter 7

The chapter centers upon Japanese views of after-hours man in his narrower behavioral environment; it says little about his role on the wider stage of world society. For two sketches of the latter, see a more academic portrait by the noted religious historian Kishimoto Hideo, "The Self-image and Aspiration of the Japanese People in the Twentieth Century," *Journal of World History* 7:1 (1962), 86–97; and a brash and lively sketch by Oda Makoto, "Third Generation Intellectual," *Atlas* 3:2 (February, 1962), 101–106.

For further glimpses of the Japanese after-hours man, the Western reader must rely upon fiction, films, and sources on popular culture cited in the notes for Chapter 6. The monthly *Asian Survey* published by the Institute of International Studies, University of California, Berkeley, frequently carries reports on current Japanese political planning. Materials on the "new religions" and their visions of the good life are contained in Harry Thomsen's recent survey, *The New Religions of Japan* (Rutland and Tokyo, 1963).

References

PAGE

162–The motto is translated from Furuta Akira, "Kojin no naka no yoka," pp. 110–126 *in Yoka*, p. 124.

163–Eda Saburō as quoted by A. M. Rosenthal, "New Policy for Japan's Socialists," *New York Times* (Western Edition), November 29, 1962.

165–Takechi's bit of science and social science fiction, "Jū-nen go no josei no seikatsu," appears in *Seikatsu no Tanoshimi*, pp. 20–32. The 1956 Japan Broadcasting Corporation survey is cited in *Yoka*, p. 44.

168–de Grazia, *Of Time, Work, and Leisure*, p. 384. W. W. Rostow, *The Stages of Economic Growth* (London and New York, 1960), esp. pp. 63–65.

169–Ōno Tsumoto, from his " 'Yoriyoi kurashi' to wa nanika," *Shisō no Kagaku* no. 17 (May, 1960):83–96; p. 83. Frank Gibney, "Japan: the New Far West," *Show* 3:5 (May, 1963) 63, 116–117, 119. David M. Potter, *People of Plenty: Economic Abundance and the American Character* (Chicago, 1954), p. 165.

171–The standard translation of the mythological "rock door" scene is W. G. Aston's, *Nihongi, Chronicles of Japan from the Earliest Times to A.D. 697* (London, 1896), vol. I, pp. 40–45.

172–On Kinokuniya and Naraya see Sheldon, *The Rise of the Merchant Class*, pp. 94–95; and Takekoshi, *The Economic Aspects*, vol. II, pp. 223–225.

173–On rates of personal savings see "Savings in the Economic Growth of Postwar Japan," *United Nations Economic Bulletin for Asia and the Far East* (Bangkok) 11,2 (1960) 1–42.

176–Dore discusses "individuation" in *City Life*, pp. 387–393.

177–Furuta, "Kojin no naka no yoka," p. 119.

178–The table appears in Takahashi Akira, "Development of Democratic Consciousness Among the Japanese People," *International Social Science Journal*, 13,1 (1960) 78–91, p. 89. Unfortunately Takahashi provides no details as to sample size, definition of "youth" and so on.

179–Okamoto Tarō, "Tsukuru koto, ajiwau koto," pp. 53–67 *in Seikatsu no Tanoshimi*, pp. 60–61. The tract "Perfect Liberty" as quoted by Thomsen, *The New Religions*, p. 194.

180–On attitudes toward being male or female, Ray E. Baber, *Youth Looks at Marriage and the Family, A Study of Changing Japanese Attitudes* (Tokyo, 1958), pp. 24–29. Studies on suicide are summarized in George A. De Vos "Deviancy and Social Change: A Psychocultural Evaluation of Trends in Japanese Delinquency and Suicide," pp. 153–171 *in* Smith and Beardsley *Japanese Culture*. Tabuse Mitsuko, "Tanoshimu Gurūpu," pp. 190–205 *in Seikatsu no Tanoshimi*, p. 202.

181–Fukutake Tadashi, *Man and Society in Japan* (Tokyo, 1962), pp. 47–48.

182–Matsumoto, *Contemporary Japan*, p. 66.

184–Figures on "stopping off" from the Tokyo University survey are given in the *Asahi Shimbun*, February 2, 1960. The other survey is cited in Yomiuri Shimbun Shakaibu (hen), *Watashi to Anata: Gendai Kazoku no Seikatsu to Iken* (Tokyo, 1962), p. 106.

185–On the "GHQ Movement" see "Boku wa konnichi koso GHQ," *Shūkan Asahi*, February 23, 1961, pp. 12–18.

186–The description of American partying is from "Boku wa konnichi koso GHQ," p. 14.

Chapter 8

Vast efforts are being turned to the comparative study of the causes of modernization. I feel that we also need to develop a formal anthropological framework for the comparative study of the effects of modernization. But that is a task for another time. The reader may be interested in carrying out a less formal comparison by examining the Japanese case as I have construed it in conjunction with the American case as nicely summarized in Samuel P. Hays, *The Response to Industrialism 1885–1914* (Chicago, 1957) and the British case as sketched by Guy Chapman, *Culture and Survival* (London, 1940). I do not know of a suitable and similarly brief study of the Soviet Union.

References
PAGE

190–The motto from Oda Makoto, "Third-Generation Intellectual," p. 106.

194–Goodman, *Growing Up Absurd* (New York, 1962), pp. 140–141.

195–Simmel from Kurt H. Wolff (transl. and ed.), *The Sociology of Georg Simmel* (Glencoe, 1950), p. 413.

Illustrations

The drawings were prepared by Mr. Yanagisawa Takeshi, a professional artist and lifelong Anchiku resident. He was born in Matsumoto in 1926, and presently resides in the city's eastern suburbs, in Sato-Yamabe. After he was graduated from higher elementary school Mr. Yanagisawa earned a livelihood as a farmer while in his after hours he taught himself drawing and painting. In 1946 he became a pupil of Seki Shirōgorō, a member of the *Shun'yōkai*, an association of prominent Japanese artists. Subsequently, Mr. Yanagisawa himself was elected to the association, and in 1962 he also was named president of the Central Nagano Art League. In recent years he has at times taught art in middle schools, and at times been employed by the Matsumoto newspaper *Shin'yō Shimbun*. He is often seen cruising about Anchiku on his motorbike in search of further subjects for his pen and brush.

The illustrations at the beginning of each chapter are as follows:

CHAPTER 1. "Matsumoto Station"—the ticket office and main waiting room in the background; before it a small portion of the station plaza at the height of the morning rush.

CHAPTER 2. "Reaping Rice"—against the backdrop of the Northern Alps, four workers are cutting the rice stalks. They use a small curved sickle with a serrated cutting edge. The woman at the lower right is binding the stalks into bunches. She wraps each bundle with a twist of dry straw taken from the cluster tied to her hip. Later the bundles will be hung to dry for a fortnight upon the long racks (not shown) mentioned in the accompanying poem. Bird-scares dangle from the lines in the middle distance.

CHAPTER 3. "Morning Departure"—in a salaryman's household. As the grandmother (background) looks on, the salaryman (business suit) takes leave of his wife (white house-apron). In the entryway at the left are a son in black school uniform, and a daughter toting her books and supplies in a knapsack.

CHAPTER 4. "Stature of Ninomiya Kinjirō"—the famous figure once so common in schoolyards, showing the boy Ninomiya studying as he carries a load of firewood.

CHAPTER 5. "Blossom Viewing"—springtime picnic under the cherry trees in a Matsumoto park. The group has spread thin straw mats, and has brought a picnic lunch (in a nest of lacquer boxes, bottom center) and bottles of sake.

CHAPTER 6. "Women's Club Meeting"—in a community People's Hall. The blackboard (for writing the meeting agenda), the low tables in hollow square, the cups of tea, are standard arrangements for meetings of this sort.

CHAPTER 7. "Apartments"—a modern steel-and-concrete apartment project in Matsumoto City, the kind of project de-

215

scribed in Chapter 2 as "Hikari ga Oka." A favored locus for the "brighter life."

CHAPTER 8. "Watching TV From the Kotatsu"—in an Anchiku home. The kotatsu is a wooden frame covered with quilts and heated inside either by a pot of charcoal or an electric coil. Feet—and often hands—are inserted under the quilts for warmth. The television receiver stands in front of the *tokonoma*, the decorative alcove commonly found in Japanese sitting rooms. At the lower left a kettle heats over a charcoal brazier, and beside it sits a teapot on a tray.

Index

219

DATE DUE